# PRAISE FOR *LEOPARD WARRIOR*

"A beautiful invitation to open your eyes and heart to whole new worlds of shamanic healing and spirit. A reminder to trust your dreams and inspiration, and to love, dance, and awaken to mystery."

JACK KORNFIELD
author of *A Path with Heart* and *A Lamp in the Darkness*

"*Leopard Warrior* is a truly remarkable account of the initiation of a white male in South Africa into becoming a sangoma. This is quite a sign, to be entrusted with these deep ancestral mysteries. John Lockley shares a wealth of stories that will bring tears to your eyes as well as inspire you to want to learn more. The exercises he provides are simple yet transformative. This book is brilliant!"

SANDRA INGERMAN, MA
author of *Soul Retrieval* and *Walking in Light:
The Everyday Empowerment of Shamanic Life*

"This is a curious but quite extraordinary story—a modern 'hero's journey' where the author reaches fulfillment as a Xhosa sangoma. Pursued as a warrior leopard might on its survival routes, this book is brimful with imagination, risk-taking, adventures of the mind, and integrity. At the core of it, there is indeed a wisdom beyond the ego, not just of 'the ancients' and ancestors, but also of now, of the heart, of the dream, of the creativity of natural things, and of Ubuntu (humanity). It is in many ways a promise for the individual in community, a poetry of life itself for everybody.

Grounded in storytelling skill and daily practice, this is a narration through philosophy and ritual in action. John's passion and questions fill his writing. The five words coming to my mind at his heart's core: energy, humanity, dreaming, action, and importantly, harmony. They belong in each of us."

SEAMUS CASHMAN
Irish author of *The Sistine Gaze: I Too Begin with Scaffolding*;
founder and former publisher at Wolfhound Press

"In our time, many non-tribal Western people are now experiencing strong dreams in which they are invited to return to the shaman's ancient spiritual path of direct revelation. The South African-born John Lockley is one such person, and his fascinating story provides us with evidence of how the tribal ancestors of his land are recruiting ambassadors outside of their lineage who can spread their wisdom and healing traditions into our troubled world. Lockley is one of those who receives messages from the spirit worlds through dreams, visions, and divination so he can serve as a bridge and give these messages to us. In *Leopard Warrior*, John Lockley lifts the veil between ignorance and wisdom and reveals how those called to the shaman's path live in the liminal spaces between the shadowlands and the light. From my own experience, this is quite an adventure."

HANK WESSELMAN, PHD
anthropologist and author of *The Re-Enchantment: The Shamanic Path to a Life of Wonder*, the award-winning *Awakening to the Spirit World* (with Sandra Ingerman), *The Bowl of Light: Ancestral Wisdom from a Hawaiian Shaman*, and the critically-acclaimed *Spiritwalker* trilogy


"From Apartheid South Africa to Korean Zen temples and Xhosa sangoma ceremonies, John Lockley takes the reader on a ride deep into the bright heart of Africa while teaching us how to connect to our blood and bones along the way. This is a unique story of a unique man's experience bringing ancient African traditions into the modern world and embodying his name: 'a bridge between peoples.'"

CHARLIE MORLEY
author of the bestselling *Dreams of Awakening*


"Like the Buddha, John was called to leave a privileged life, drawn inexorably into rigorous training in Xhosa shamanism and Korean Zen meditation. His gorgeous writing invites us to come along on his extraordinary journey, taking a deep breath of Zen as we feel the heartbeat of our shared humanity—of Africa, our ancestors, and Mother Nature as a doorway into our true nature."

TRUDY GOODMAN, PHD
founding teacher of InsightLA

"It was when I was researching about intercultural communication in post-apartheid South Africa that I came across John Lockley's work. I asked myself a question that many black South Africans have: How can a white man become a Xhosa sangoma? That question is answered in this book as John describes his personal experiences undergoing traditional Zen training and a sangoma apprenticeship. In detailed, easy-to-understand language, John has painted a picture of 'Ubuntuism' in post-apartheid South Africa. I find it very important as we are still grappling with issues of transformation in South Africa."

DR. HLEZE KUNJU, PHD
isiXhosa linguist, Sol Plaatje University, Northern Cape, South Africa

"Before I met John Lockley, I heard him in a dream, drumming non-stop. The next morning, meeting him for the first time in waking life, I knew he was the real deal—a Xhosa sangoma. In this wonderful and readable book, John builds a bridge to an ancient tradition of depth, compassion, and mystery. Through his stories and lessons, you will discover the Xhosa path of connecting to a deeper sense of humanity, healing, and heartfelt awareness."

ROBERT WAGGONER
author of *Lucid Dreaming: Gateway to the Inner Self*

"This is a rich and absorbing account of how a white South African found meaning and his life's work in an indigenous spirituality from the Xhosa tradition. John's story is an inspiration for all who attempt to live consciously in the world of dreams, ancestors, and magic. If you wonder about how a modern man can authentically embody an ancient spirituality in the contemporary world, don't miss this important book."

TOM COWAN
author of *Fire in the Head: Shamanism and the Celtic Spirit* and
*Yearning for the Wind: Celtic Reflections on Nature and the Soul*

"Beautifully articulated and evocatively expressed. This is a captivating autobiography of one man's remarkable journey from affliction, suffering, and pain in racially-torn South Africa to healing, redemption, and spiritual attuning through an intriguing combination of Zen Buddhism, African healing spirituality, and Irish ancestral inspiration. With deep and respectful sincerity for the wisdom and generosity of his healing guides, John offers simple and effective ways in which seekers of healing can honor their ancestors, listen to their dreams, and bring about a transformation of self."

DR. PENNY BERNARD, PHD
anthropologist at Rhodes University, Grahamstown, South Africa

"John Lockley is a white man that can dance! And he plays the skin drum like he was born to it. This is an extraordinary tale of a middle-class South African who had the dreaded African 'calling sickness.' To heal, he went through years of rigorous traditional African spiritual training and ritual sacrifice. With great eloquence and sensitivity, John relates his wild journey, which takes him from his life as a Zen student in the East, to his mystical studies in Ireland, to eventually becoming an African sangoma. He combines his life's work of spirit hunting in the brave and profound teachings he calls The Way of the Leopard."

CRAIG FOSTER
award-winning South African documentary filmmaker of
the films *My Hunter's Heart, The Great Dance, A Hunter's
Story, Cosmic Africa*, and *The Animal Communicator*

"The stars moved and shifted to call John Lockley to the path of The Dancing Healer, to carrying on the sangoma tradition. While working with my teaching partner Antoinette Spillane and me, we could see his warrior's heart, respect, and dedication to the earth-based and ancient culture of healing through dance, movement, voice, music, and sacred ritual. John safely opens the door into the unconscious and the dreamtime using an embodied tribal structure that has been tried and tested for thousands of years. This work is vital, for ourselves, our families, and the changing heart of the planet."

LANI O' HANLON
Irish author of *Dancing the Rainbow: Holistic Well-Being through Movement*

"This is a lovely and important book. In it, John Lockley describes his chronic illness and loneliness as a young white man in apartheid South Africa, and how this suffering was given meaning in the sangoma tradition of the Xhosa people. It follows his long apprenticeship and initiation, as well as his struggles to communicate this way of healing in a traumatized world. John seamlessly combines his years of Zen practice with his calling as a sangoma, and he uses them together to live in the service of others. The book is written with gratitude and without pretension; it is a reminder of the great commitment required for the path that has chosen him, and of his determination to be a builder of bridges between all that divides us. I was deeply touched by it. Camagu, Cingo, Camagu!"

ANTONY OSLER (DAE CHONG, OSHO)
South African human rights advocate; author of *Stoep Zen:
A Zen Life in South Africa, Zen Dust: A Journey Home
Through the Back Roads of South Africa*, and *Mzansi Zen*

"John Lockley has surpassed all of my expectations in his new book *Leopard Warrior*. I run a non-profit that is dedicated to the conservation of indigenous cultures and their wisdom. Working with John, I have watched his sincere dedication to the sangoma traditions manifest before my eyes, and since reading his book, I realize the deep sadness, commitment, and pain he has endured to become a sangoma in the Xhosa tradition. His humbleness and deep regard for his teachers shines out on every page, and the deeper understanding of the rich spirit and ceremony of his people may bring the shaking to your soul. This book is masterfully written along with the ancestors and dreams that guide his own spirit. I often felt deeply the emotional ride it was for him to triumph in his calling."

PATRICIA TURNER
founder of Tierra Sagrada, The Sacred Earth Foundation

# LEOPARD WARRIOR

18/14/2017.

Dear Mark,

Thanks for a great show today.
I hope my book can inspire you
to deepen your Dreaming.

Best Wishes,

John x

JOHN LOCKLEY

# LEOPARD WARRIOR

A Journey into the African Teachings
of Ancestry, Instinct, and Dreams

sounds true
BOULDER, COLORADO

Sounds True
Boulder, CO 80306

Published 2017

Cover design by Jennifer Miles
Book design by Beth Skelley

Cover image © Galyna Andrushko, pattern © Liza Ievleva
All photos and illustrations are courtesy of the author unless otherwise noted.

Printed in Canada

Library of Congress Cataloging-in-Publication Data
Names: Lockley, John, author.
Title: Leopard warrior : a journey into the African teachings of ancestry,
   instinct, and dreams / John Lockley.
Description: Boulder : Sounds True, Inc., 2017. | Includes bibliographical
   references.
Identifiers: LCCN 2017008150 (print) | LCCN 2017032998 (ebook) |
   ISBN 9781622039043 (ebook) | ISBN 9781622039036 (pbk.)
Subjects: LCSH: Xhosa (African people—Religion. | Shamanism—South Africa. |
   Zen Buddhism—South Africa. | Lockley, John. | Shamans—South Africa—
   Biography. | Ubuntu (Philosophy)
Classification: LCC BL2480.X55 (ebook) | LCC BL2480.X55 L63 2017 (print) |
   DDC 299.6/83985—dc23
LC record available at https://lccn.loc.gov/2017008150

10 9 8 7 6 5 4 3 2 1

This book is dedicated to my Mom and Dad, who stood by me through hard times and showed me the meaning of unconditional love, and to my beloved teachers MaMngwevu and Tat' uSukwini, who taught me the true meaning of *ubunzulu bobuntu*—the depth of humanity.

# Contents

# Foreword

A few years ago I crossed paths with a strange-looking, extremely white man dressed like an exotic sangoma priest. Looking at him, I wondered what kind of turbulent journey could have possibly marooned him into this "mess" and what shaman could have managed to drag this white man into a tradition not of his ancestry. He wore his status quite elegantly and devotedly, with an edge to militancy, as if he had made up his mind that the tradition he embodied was an integral part of his identity. I was indeed struck by his humility, as he appeared to carry the demeanor of the sage with dignity.

Needless to say, I was fascinated by this tall blond young man who looked as if he had freshly returned from the other world. Who wouldn't be? I badly needed to hear his story, but I didn't know how to ask. Fortunately, I didn't have to. He let me read it.

John Lockley's story is a remarkable and fascinating testimony to the ways in which the African ancestors pick and choose who they want to be the voice of their wisdom in the world. He is evidence that the ancestors have gone outside the tribal lineage to recruit ambassadors who can spread their wisdom and healing traditions. John's story is a captivating testimony of a hero's journey into uncharted territories.

It began on a humid August night, several decades ago, in Johannesburg, South Africa. John woke up from a startlingly vivid dream that would change the course of his life indelibly. He had clearly been summoned to become a Xhosa sangoma.

There are certain dreams you cannot ignore. This is partly because ancestral calls to duty are not interested in your prior plans, not to mention your opinion, and do not come with the kind of umbrella of safety one would naturally want in the interest of predictability and comfort. There may have been a resistance in him, but whether there was or not, John suffered the ordeal consistent with his calling as part of his initiation. It came as a burning fever, an excruciating pain, as the spirit rewired him for the job of his life. In these moments of dismantling, one cannot see the light. Initiation is a brush with uncertainty, danger, and death. It fosters depression and bewilderment. Trapped in a country rigged by apartheid while knowing he had to find a sangoma willing to mentor him, the eighteen-year-old middle-class student could not have found a more difficult path to follow. But it happened. As apartheid ended, he found a remarkable senior Xhosa sangoma named MaMngwevu to help him walk his newly assigned path. Teachers and students are often called to one another. This was one such case; his teacher knew him before they met for the first time.

*Leopard Warrior* is an account of the wealth of ancestral wisdom entrusted to John by his saintly teacher over more than a decade. It reads like a piece of literature, carefully unveiling the hidden myster-ies of Africa. This timely piece is a gift to the world that adds African wisdom to the great concert of indigenous wisdom the West so sorely needs. In it we find the colorful journey of a white man from apartheid South Africa whose studies with Nelson Mandela's medicine people highlight the humanity in us all.

Anyone interested in indigenous philosophy will find the clear and open pathway of *Ubuntu* (humanity) presented here with humility. Ubuntu emphasizes the sanctity of ancestral honoring—a unique practice in Africa that is a gift to mankind. For the last few years, prominent academics have maintained that the entire human race is descended from one small tribe in Southern Africa. John recalls an ancient Xhosa saying: "We all have red blood." He teaches that ances-tral veneration means going back in time to remember our common roots. In Xhosa spirituality, if we go back far enough, we believe that all people are related.

There is a profound hunger in the Western world for meaning and a sense of rootedness. John's teachings on Xhosa spirituality contribute a soothing touch to this longing. His Xhosa name is Cingolweendaba, meaning "messenger or bridge between people," and he has demon-strated this in a remarkable way: by traveling to the West over the past nine years spreading the Xhosa medicine teachings of *ubunzulu bobuntu* (depth of humanity). These teachings attempt to bridge the gap between the Western world's incredible material wealth and its psychological pain—widespread depression and an endless list of other ills—among other problems.

The healing of the West may be the job of the very cultures it looks down upon. Can Africa's material poverty meet Western spiritual barrenness to bring balance to the world? We must dream the impossible, seek the beauty of sharing wisdom through the cracks of our longing, and usher into reality the possibility of a world village bound together by a concert of wisdom.

John is an artisan of this and more. His work deserves respect and reverence.

**Malidoma Somé**
Dagara medicine man and elder
author, *Of Water and the Spirit*

# Author's Note

Dear Friend,

At this time in the world of delicate rebalancing in the relationships of races and cultures, I feel it is important for me to mention that I, as a South African man, was invited by Xhosa tribal elders to train to become a sangoma, a traditional South African shaman.

The Xhosa elders recognized my sangoma gift as evidenced by my dreams and further confirmed by their own dreams about me. They welcomed me in as family and were not perturbed in the least by my white skin or the fact that I am not a native Xhosa man. I apprenticed for ten years under my teacher, MaMngwevu, a senior sangoma in the Xhosa nation. She hails from the same nation as Nelson Mandela and Archbishop Desmond Tutu. And I was fortunate to experience the same sense of *Ubuntu* (humanity) from my Xhosa elders that shone from these illustrious leaders, making them so loved around the world.

My elders' trust in me and in the dreams we experienced together has laid the foundation for my "ubunzulu bobuntu," or depth of humanity teachings. These beautiful teachings added to my Zen training and inspired me to create my The Way of the Leopard teachings, which I now share worldwide. It speaks about humanity united through a symphony of blood, bones, ancestors, and dreams. It is clear that we all have red blood, and through recognizing our intrinsic humanity, anything is possible.

Please join me while I share my story with you.

Warmest wishes,
John

# Prologue

For more than seven years I had been battling the *thwasa* illness, a mysterious condition that affected my body, mind, and spirit. No matter how much I ate, I lost weight. I was plagued by terrifying nightmares. As my body grew weaker and weaker, I fell victim to one ailment after another, some of them very grave. I spent those years in pain, fear, and confusion, unable to explain why I could never completely recover from one illness before another struck me. Western medicine had no answers for me.

I didn't yet know that I had the "calling illness," which had been precipitated by a powerful dream—I was so sick because I had been called to become a sangoma[1], a traditional South African shaman and healer. But this was uncharted territory. I was a middle-class white student who had grown up in South Africa in the era of apartheid. Black and white people were forced to live separately, and the sangoma tradition and lineages were exclusively black. Even if I had known what my illness meant, and that apprenticing to a senior sangoma held the cure, I would not have been able to follow that path. Had I tried to enter any of the black townships where the sangomas practiced their healing arts, I would have been questioned relentlessly by the police and armed forces. And had I persisted, it is likely I would have been arrested and imprisoned.

I don't like to think about what might have happened to me if the apartheid system had not collapsed under the weight of its cruelty and injustice. But end it did, and in 1994, with Nelson Mandela now president of South Africa, a series of events, strong dreams, and persistent intuitive messages led me at last to the divination room of MaMngwevu, a powerful senior sangoma in the Xhosa tradition, the same culture as Mandela. My body shook as I sat before her on the floor. To my side sat a translator of the isiXhosa language.

Electrical impulses of deep knowing cascaded down my spine as MaMngwevu described my long years of illness—accurately and in detail—saying how lonely I felt inside and how some days I just wanted to die. I simply nodded, overcome with emotion as I took in the smells of strong herbs and the sight of animal skins hanging from ochre-colored walls. Then MaMngwevu stopped speaking and simply looked at me. Her eyes pierced through to my soul, and in that moment there was no MaMngwevu or John Lockley. There was just the divining wind flowing like water between us.

"What took you so long to come to me?" MaMngwevu asked.

"Apartheid, Mama," I answered.

"*Ahh, Thixo, Nkosi yam, siphantse saphulukana nawe!*" MaMngwevu said, her voice brimming with pain and concern as tears slid down her cheeks.

I turned to my translator.

"She says, 'Oh Lord, my God, we almost lost you!'"

# Introduction

I am an *igqirha elikhulu*, a senior sangoma in the Xhosa tradition, the lineage of Nelson Mandela and Desmond Tutu. I am also a white man, the son of a Catholic mother from Ireland and a Protestant father from Rhodesia (now Zimbabwe). When I was growing up, I had no idea what a sangoma was or what they did. If I thought of traditional African healers at all, I thought of them as "witch doctors" trading in magic and superstition. The colonial culture in which I lived had done a good job of planting and reinforcing those false ideas. To be clear, we are spiritual messengers. Our job is actually simple—to receive messages from the spirit world through dreams, waking visions, or divination and give these messages to the people. We are metaphysicians: soul doctors. We help people connect with their inner worlds and thereby find harmony and balance with the outer world. We see all illness as a call to connect with our inner nature, or authentic selves.

I was born in 1971 into a world at war: South Africa under apartheid, one of the worst forms of social engineering the world has ever seen; Zimbabwe (Rhodesia at that time) experiencing civil war; and Northern Ireland in flames during the time of sectarian strife known as the Troubles. In South Africa, people were segregated based on the color of their skin, with white people given preferential treatment in work, education, and living space. Yet no one is completely white, and how white are we all inside? Color is only skin deep. In the deepest parts of us—beyond culture, religion, and gender—we are all the same. We are human beings with a divine mission: to help one another. In isiXhosa we say, "*Uthando luthando*." (Love is love.) And after years of spiritual pilgrimage and training, I added a second phrase, "*Ubuntu luthando*." (Humanity is love.)

I was born with white birth skin around my eyes. This, according to my Xhosa teacher, is the mark of a Xhosa sangoma. Seeing this as I took my first breath, my mother exclaimed in her Dublin accent, "He looks like an abo!"—an aboriginal Australian. I am told the white doctor frowned, my dad laughed, and the black Xhosa nursing sisters ululated.

## SEARCHING FOR PEACE

The first eighteen years of my life were about me finding my vision and place in the world—a white child with an indigenous calling, growing to manhood while navigating an alien and troubled world. White middle-class men were supposed to be lawyers, doctors, and psychologists, not witch doctors or shamans. Yet I dreamed. My dreams were about the African bushveld, animals, and plants, about illness and healing. Meanwhile, I absorbed the social disharmony of both my mother's homeland and my beloved yet torn South Africa. Conflict and transformation became familiar friends to me. I breathed them in—a bitter pill that I longed to expel. I yearned for peace the way a starving man yearns for food.

My search for peace became a living pilgrimage as I traveled the world working with healers, mystics, psychics, Zen masters, and shamans. South Korean Buddhism opened its doors to me, teaching me the beauty and simplicity of Zen, while Southern Africa taught me about the magical realm of my birth: sangoma medicine. And Ireland taught me that laughter and music are a living story that never ends.

## THE CALL TO WRITE THIS BOOK

I wrote this story in hopes that I would inspire people to follow their dreams, ancestors, and spiritual calling. The book describes my personal experiences undergoing traditional Zen training and a sangoma apprenticeship. I by no means hold myself as an authority on either tradition, and I do not presume to direct anyone else's spiritual journey. Following a spiritual calling is a deeply personal experience. We must listen for our own unique path, with the same fascination and awe we experience when we hear a newborn baby's cry or feel an ocean breeze.

When I discussed my idea of writing this book with my Xhosa elders in South Africa's Eastern Cape, I told them that I wouldn't share the secrets of our tradition, that my calling to write it was to help people connect with their ancestors and dreams. They listened to me with great compassion and kindness and gave me their full and unanimous support.

I told them that many people in the Western world have forgotten their ancestors and don't know how to connect with them. They received this news quietly. Among traditional South African people, it is considered the duty of every human being to honor and remember their ancestors. To forget one's people represents a sadness beyond words. If we forget where we come from, we become spiritually lost. We undermine our Ubuntu—our humanity—and our ability to navigate life with the compass of our hearts rather than just our egos. This is important to understand because when we are connected to our roots, it becomes possible for us to bear fruit in the world, to shine and connect with our calling, our life path. The state of war on our planet represents the inner turmoil of millions of people disconnected from their roots.

To change a glass of water into a healing elixir requires only a few drops of good medicine. The medicine I teach—and that I will share with you in these pages—is how to connect to your own blood and bones. If you realize that you are the embodiment of your ancestors and represent all their hopes and dreams, you will spread peace and harmony. Your stream of peace will feed into a river of peace, and the river will gather momentum as more and more people practice this medicine.

Every human being, no matter how rich or poor, has an effect on our collective humanity. We all have a responsibility to listen to our hearts and dreams and to honor our forebears. As we do this, we will wake up and manifest the dreams of our ancestors.

## THE WAY OF THE LEOPARD

The leopard is a sacred animal in traditional African healing circles. It is one of our main animal totems and represents intuition, instinct, harmony with nature, and the spirit world. It embodies the characteristics of nature: wild, unpredictable, sublimely intelligent—and sometimes dangerous. And like sangomas everywhere, it occupies the twilight world, coming alive with the first and last glimmer of light, the time when sangomas pray. Leopards are also fiercely independent and travel alone, using their senses to navigate the world. Some sangomas work independently like the leopard and are sent into distant regions to open people to the wonders of the spirit world. This has been my calling, and one of my sangoma names is Indlu Yengwe, meaning "house of the leopard." It was given to me by the Zulu sage and master sangoma Credo Mutwa in recognition of my work in bringing sacred African teachings to the Western world.[1]

The Way of the Leopard™ is what I call my teachings to help people find their own strength and calling in the world and to connect to their seven senses: the five physical senses as well as the sixth, perception, and the seventh, dreams. To do this in a powerful way, we are called on to become like warriors, fiercely courageous in the instinctual pursuit of our own dreams and connection to both the spirit world and nature. The leopard warrior is a spiritual soldier, forged by nature, seeking a way to awaken all their senses.

A key theme throughout this book is reconnecting with your ancestors and the forces of nature. As you do this in a mindful way, you

John and Credo Mutwa, 2008.

naturally open your senses and increase your ability to dream and make sense of your life purpose. When you follow your calling, you experience a greater sense of inner contentment and harmony. I believe that when many people practice The Way of the Leopard—becoming leopard warriors in their own right—the result will be stronger, more cohesive communities, and hopefully less war.

This story is about Ubuntu and how we can find a way to go beyond prejudice and hatred to a place of peace, beauty, and togetherness. I use the leopard as a colorful metaphor, a creature in harmony with itself and the world around it. Each morning as the leopard wakes, it scratches and licks itself clean and then begins the process of searching for food. Like the leopard lying on a branch in the light of an African dawn, we start with an inner journey, first waking our senses and then engaging with our communities and nature.

## HOW THIS BOOK IS ORGANIZED

The book follows a chronological sequence. It begins with my work as a hospital medic in a black special forces ward and my first realization that I could be accepted among black South Africans. It weaves through my training in Zen Buddhism, which became my anchor as I navigated the rough seas of the thwasa illness before meeting my Xhosa teacher. I share that meeting, as well as some of what I have generally learned about Xhosa culture and mysticism. I describe my ten-year apprenticeship and the three main elements of my work as a sangoma: dancing, herbalism, and divination. And I recount my initiation as a full sangoma and my subsequent travels around the world as a practicing sangoma. Finally, I share with you some of the essential practices that I have developed—a blending of Zen and Xhosa wisdom streams—so you too can learn the techniques that have been transformational for many of my students and clients.

Here is my story. Please read it with an open mind and with sensitivity. I am sharing my dreams with you so that you might walk the road of your spirit and realize your life's calling.

May your dreams be clear and your heart open like the wind.

# PART I

Dreamtime

# 1

# Blood and Tears

They came in tatters, their bodies and minds ravaged by war and life in a society where nothing was equal and nothing made sense. These were soldiers from the war in Angola that had raged for more than ten years, a Southern African "Vietnam" on a colossal scale.[1] They arrived in droves at 1 Military Hospital in Voortrekkerhoogte, Pretoria, South Africa, and it was my job to help heal them.

The year was 1990 and I was an eighteen-year-old soldier, a draftee, in the South African army.[2] I had chosen to be a medic because I abhorred war—I wanted to learn how to heal, not kill. I was working in the rehabilitation unit, Ward 13, making sure that all the men's needs were addressed. Most of them had posttraumatic stress; in their minds they were still fighting. The majority of my patients were black special forces soldiers. It was from them that I first learned about traditional African culture and the meaning of Ubuntu: humanity.

The soldiers faced a double war: Angola outside South Africa and civil war within. Black people countrywide were in revolt against the scourge, the inhumanity, of apartheid.

Apartheid is an Afrikaans word meaning "separate development,"[3] and the different racial groups in South Africa were given different places to live. This made it difficult for most black South Africans to rise above the status of working class. The black majority had been pushed into subservience and disenfranchised. Standing up to the South African government, they rioted and held mass rallies. It became particularly painful and problematic when black soldiers were sent into African townships after fighting in Angola, forced to turn against their own people.[4]

One Military Hospital offered a brief sanctuary and reprieve from the volcano of socio-political unrest on the streets outside. Within its corridors we did our best to heal the physical bodies of the soldiers, but the complicated social issues were in the hands of the politicians, and all we could do was hope, pray, and dream about a better country for all.

At first, every day I walked into the black soldiers' room, threw open the curtains, and said without thinking, "Morning, guys. Did you have any good dreams?" And every day I was answered with silence. Then, on the third day, a well-respected sergeant from the Recces, an elite special forces unit,[5] called out to me, "Private, come over here. I want to speak to you!"

I approached him.

"Private," he said, "in our culture dreams are sacred. When I dream, my ancestors show me who is going to live and who is going to die in my platoon. I tell my men. Some of them laugh at me, and they still die. I have learned to be careful with my dreams, and only tell people if they are really listening."

Sergeant Ndlovu was Zulu and an apprenticing sangoma, a traditional healer and medicine man. I thanked him for his teaching. I had noticed that the black nursing sisters respectfully came and talked to him each day. Sergeant Ndlovu taught me my first lesson in South African mysticism, and the more I watched and listened to him and his surrounding soldier brothers, the more I learned about African culture and spirituality.

Soldiers who bragged and complained about pain often had little to actually complain about. Those who were quiet, with an aura of mindful focus around them, frequently had very serious injuries, such as amputations and complicated compound fractures. Often, the complaining patients were white soldiers and the quiet ones were black, silently going about the meticulous business of healing their bodies. On a number of occasions, our senior consultant, Colonel Gordon, noted with admiration and medical curiosity that his black patients healed three times faster than his white patients. Many people considered Dr. Gordon an ardent racist and a supporter of apartheid, yet he was a good doctor and was typical of the contradictions endemic in the country at the time. He always asked me how his special forces soldiers were and referred to each by name, and he made sure that we had enough vitamin supplements and the special vitamin A and E creams that helped heal the skin from abrasions and injuries. I noticed that only the black men used these creams. Whites considered them "sissy," but my black patients were oblivious to these sentiments.

An undercurrent in all our ward rounds was wondering how these black guys healed so quickly. Yet because we lived under apartheid, we never openly discussed the question. We didn't discuss apartheid itself either, but in my heart I knew its end was near. I was determined to solve the riddle of my black patients' rapid healing, even from horrendous injuries such as amputations and from untold hardship. In them, I observed a steady acceptance of life.

When my African patients rubbed their bodies with vitamin creams, it was like a meditation to them—and they applied them from head to foot! When I went home, I rubbed my body with the same stuff. My father would look at me and then at my mother and say, "Yonnie, you are making a woman out of my son!" Once, in response, I said, "Dad, if these creams are good enough for special forces soldiers, they are good enough for me!" He made no further comments. I continued to use the creams in the same meditative way I had observed. Years later when I had my own injuries, this experience of using body creams helped facilitate my healing.

War was evident on the faces of the men. Their bodies were healing, but their minds were preoccupied with their experiences in Angola. When I tried to talk about it with some of the special forces soldiers I had befriended, I was greeted with grim smiles. "Ag, John, it was complicated there, my friend," replied Diego Santos, my Portuguese-speaking friend who had been brought up in a mission station in Angola. When I asked him why he had joined the army, he said he had very little choice. It offered him food, education, medicine, clothing, and safety for his family. If he hadn't joined, the guerrilla forces would have taken him—by force—and he would have had to fight anyway, without proper education, medicine, or training. Most likely, he said, he would have been killed by the South African forces. So he enlisted.

One evening I stole three beers from the officers' mess, and Diego and I drank them while the sounds of the hospital abated and the other soldiers slept. For the first time, I saw him soften and relax. If he hadn't been a soldier, he could have been a poet or musician, for his spirit was gentle, calm, and powerful. There was humility about him, like that of a priest who has spent many years in meditation. I believed this quality was what sharpened his instincts and kept him alive. Diego was used to being on his own, and he had the resilience of a leopard in the bush. Special forces soldiers were trained to survive alone behind enemy lines for long periods of time. Diego was this kind of man.

Dusk was an eerie time on the wards. The hospital felt like a battleship setting sail for the world of dreams and forgotten spirits. I could hear the murmurs of men talking in their sleep and feel other presences descend on the ward: the lost soldiers coming back from the dead to be with their comrades who were resting, recovering, or dying.

The time it took Corporal Diego to finish his two beers was the time it took for me to transition from childhood into adulthood. He told stories of courage, pain, war, and dignity. He taught me about the resilience of the human spirit. He taught me what it means to be a leopard warrior, long before I became one myself.

Many other soldiers touched my heart and made me feel the sharp pain and joy of being alive. Private Sebastian De Valera had been a foot soldier in Angola when a land mine exploded beneath him, bringing him to the brink of death and taking both his legs. He was a twenty-two-year-old Angolan, with the body of a world-class athlete, who never complained or demanded much. He enjoyed the simple, wondrous things in life, especially listening to music. I saw him cry only once, when someone stole his radio. This had a dramatic effect on the men of the ward, and they pooled their money to buy him another radio. We were all moved by Sebastian's fortitude and gentleness.

I sometimes had the pleasure of pushing Sebastian in his wheelchair out to the helipad where the casualties were flown in. When the sun was shining brightly and a soft breeze was blowing, you would think we were both at the beach. Sebastian often wore a beatific smile, and I wondered why, since he was only twenty-two and a double amputee. But after a while I understood. He was happy to be alive!

The highlight of my time in Ward 13 came one day when we had a special delivery: two new titanium legs designed and fitted especially for Sebastian. When he first put them on and I asked if I could help him walk, he shook his head and stood up straight, reached for the railing on the wall—and walked. It was the walk of freedom; his spirit soared like an eagle released from a cage. His spine was straight and dignified, and he walked slowly and deliberately, with athletic grace.

Sebastian was different from that day on. His recovery moved with lightning speed, and it wasn't too long before he was transferred from our rehabilitation ward. But the memory of that first walk has never left me.

All the medics were nervous one day when we were told that a soldier from the legendary 32 Battalion would be staying with us. This was an elite infantry regiment, nicknamed the "Buffalo Battalion," that was sent into the worst fighting situations. During the height of apartheid, the government was heavily criticized for ordering the 32 Battalion into some townships experiencing unrest. The 32's members were merciless in quelling insurrection.[6]

Private Sipho Dlamini was a Zulu man of twenty-two years with an aura of strength verging on arrogance. He knew what his body was capable of, and he moved through the ward as if it had no walls. He had very little respect for authority, which had resulted in his demotion from corporal to private. When he first arrived, every day I said hello to him and every day he completely ignored me. Soon I stopped greeting him and just watched him from afar and monitored his healing. I was aware of Sipho observing me too, and I wasn't sure if it was with hostility or not. Then one day while I was working at my desk, I saw a shadow move over my papers. The hair rose on the back of my neck, and I felt someone standing next to me with the intensity of a lion.

I stood up and turned quickly to face my assailant. There stood Private Sipho, tall, deliberate, and ready to pounce. He looked me square in the eyes and said, "Medic, I have been watching you for these last few weeks. I have seen how you treat us black guys here in the ward. You are different from the other medic, who is a racist fucker!"

His lips quivered, and I could see the anger in his eyes as I watched his neck muscles bulge. I still wasn't sure if he was going to strike me or not, and I was readying myself. But then he added, "You treat all of us with respect and you don't see color. From today you are my friend. If you have any problems with anyone, don't hesitate to come to me and I will deal with them for you. Okay?"

We shook hands, he laughed heartily, and from that day on we talked about life. That was a turning point for me. For the first time, I felt *seen*. My love and respect for my fellow soldiers had been acknowledged. I felt a renewed optimism in my role as a medic, but above all I had crossed over into the land of black Africa where I was regarded as a friend and could walk without the curse of being white. This was the start of my life-changing journey.

Sergeant Ndlovu's teaching early on about dreaming had pierced my soul and awakened inner truths that I couldn't walk away from. I too had been called in my dreams by the spirit of Africa. Beginning in 1988, I had experienced a number of profound dreams. In one of them I was searching for gold in South America. When I woke up it was clear to me that the gold was a metaphor for alchemy or spiritual transformation. The goal was finding God, enlightenment, spiritual peace, or a sense of knowing one's connection to all things. An inner voice told me that in order to find my destiny, I had to come close to death, for when we are faced with our mortality, humility is born and teaches us who we are.

I hungered to learn more about medicine and do more intensive nursing, to work with people who were dying or at death's door. An inner knowing was propelling me in this direction. I wanted to make a difference. I asked the matron of the hospital, Mrs. Potgieter, for a transfer to the intensive care unit. She was shocked. "This is the first time I have heard of a conscripted soldier who wants to do more work, not less!" she said. A few days later, I was told that the ICU was full but there was a place in Ward 8, the neurology unit.

In Ward 8 I learned about the business of nursing, from caring for the critically ill to helping patients on their way to recovery. Within a few days of arriving, I helped another medic put a soldier into a body bag. The ward was medically intense, and I found this exhilarating. It gave me many opportunities to learn. I befriended a few younger conscripted doctors, and we discussed medical situations and head injuries on our tea breaks. I read through medical journals. I learned how to perform basic nursing procedures. A few of my patients had tracheostomy tubes running from their trachea to their lungs to help with their breathing, so I learned how to clean them. This was an intricate process that required concentration, a steady hand, and kindness.

One of the patients I was assigned to was twenty-two-year-old Emmanuel, and his case was the toughest I ever had to deal with. Emmanuel had been injured when an army truck he was traveling in overturned. Almost every bone in his body was broken and he was in a semicoma. We waited for him to join us, but he never really did. Although his eyes were open, we were not sure whether he had any recognition of his surroundings. Every day his mother came into the ward and sat by his side, and every day she asked me, "Do you think he is getting any better?" I replied, "Yes, slowly but surely!" But I was lying. I wanted to be kind to her; the truth was unthinkable.

I nursed Emmanuel for more than six weeks. Every day I took his pulse, tested his reflexes, and cleaned his tracheostomy tube. As gentle as I was, it was still uncomfortable for him, and sometimes he had convulsive fits and phlegm from his lungs sprayed upward like an erupting volcano. I felt these fits were his way of saying, "I am still here!" I spoke to him because I believed that some part of him still knew what was going on. He got one infection after another, and we all did our best to ease his suffering. In quiet moments we could hear him grinding his teeth: the methodical gnashing of a young man whose life had been cut short. That was all he could do to express his profound frustration.

It became harder and harder to find his pulse. I pressed my fingers on his temple until I could feel the quiet sigh of his heartbeat. As his condition worsened and his infections grew stronger, the medical team of Ward 8 met with Emmanuel's family. They decided to turn off the machines that were preserving his life, a life that had become reduced to infinite suffering. Emmanuel's was the hardest case in the whole ward, and when I spoke to one of the older medics, he said he had never experienced such a sad one.

We all struggled to hold back tears, from the toughest specialists to the medical orderlies like myself, and stood by Emmanuel's side as he started to die. The more senior medics found it too difficult to stand by his side and take his vital observations every fifteen to twenty minutes, so they asked me to do it. It was an honor to be by his side. Life is sacred, and each time I touched his temple to feel his heartbeat it felt like a prayer. Each time I left his room I felt the beauty of life and how lucky we all were not to be experiencing Emmanuel's pain. Yet I was incredibly frustrated I couldn't do more. We had the best that modern Western medicine had to offer, but we couldn't save Emmanuel and we couldn't ease his family's heartache.

My shift was about to end, and I knew that when I returned, Emmanuel would be dead. Just before I left his room, I watched him from afar, family and medical staff gathered around him, a small group of loved ones. I felt the heavy sadness of it all.

I prayed earnestly and inwardly. *God, all this suffering is just not right! I call on all the angels and saints in this world. I call on Jesus, I call on Mary, I call on all that is holy and good in this world. Please bear witness to this suffering. Please show me another way to heal, so that if I am ever in this position again, I can do something.* I closed the door behind me and walked out of the ward. The next day when I returned for duty, Emmanuel's room was empty.

Emmanuel's death proved a great turning point in my life. And just as my prophetic dream about searching for gold foretold, the sharpness of death helped me realize my destiny.

# 2

# The Calling Dream

Afterr my fervent prayer in Emmanuel's hospital room, the universe soon conspired to help me find answers to the riddle of suffering that was all around me. The first part of the answer came in the form of Zen Buddhism.

If you are unfamiliar with it, Buddhism was founded more than two thousand years ago by an Indian prince named Siddhartha Gautama. Siddhartha lived an insulated life of comfort and pleasure until one day he left his palace and entered the nearby village—and was struck to the core by the suffering of the villagers. The next day he set out on a journey, determined to find an answer to the existential questions "Who am I?" and "Why do we suffer so much on this earth plane?" Legend has it that after six years of meditating, he achieved supreme enlightenment while sitting under a Bodhi tree and devoted the rest of his life to helping people find answers to these age-old questions.

I was first attracted to the Japanese Zen form of Buddhism because of its simplicity, clarity, and its pursuit of answers to "Who am I?" "What is suffering?" and "Why do we eat every day?" It tackled these questions with Samurai discipline. Its main practices are meditation, chanting, and bowing, and these were a soothing balm for my spirit. I was taught by a lay nun named Onesan, a disciple of the Japanese Zen Master Taisen Deshimaru, whose classes I attended on my days off from the army. In meditation I learned to focus on my breathing and my center, about two inches below the belly button, and found the practice both energizing and calming. In the beginning I sat in meditation every day for twenty minutes, a period that stretched over the years to an hour.

My life moved quickly after my urgent prayer. Within two months of Emmanuel's death I found myself traveling to my first Zen retreat in the Tzaneen forest in the Northern Transvaal province of South Africa. After a harrowing plane ride on a cold, misty evening that made me wonder if the universe might be checking on just how calm and Zen I really was, Onesan's husband, Patrick, picked me up and we drove into the heart of the Tzaneen forest. I felt I was on a mystical quest mirroring my first dreams at seventeen. I remember thinking, *This is going to be big for me. Something is going to shift. Something huge is about to happen.*

The forest was vibrant, and I rejoiced in the bittersweetness of life. I was happy; my reason for living was going to be made apparent to me. I was sure that all the suffering I had seen and experienced had not been in vain. It was leading me to a direct reflection of the "moment world." My fellow soldiers had taught me about the brevity of life, and my Zen practice had shown me how to focus my mind and breath. So now the work at hand was to "just be," to savor each moment and wait for destiny to reveal itself.

A few days later, back in Johannesburg, I had an epic dream that would change my life completely. I termed this my "calling dream."

I woke up in an ancient world that felt tangible and startlingly real. I was in a very dark place, like a cave, lying on my belly on the ground. The space smelled of herbs. On my right was a young black man about my age. We were both lying naked and outstretched before our teacher, as is the practice in a traditional sangoma apprenticeship.

Our teacher was a "witch doctor" with beautiful, shining eyes, black skin, and animal skins draped around his body. I was speaking to him with my mind. I said, "Teach me about nature, about suffering, everything!"

I was answered with a profound silence.

When I asked again, I was met with more silence.

Then I asked a third time and heard his voice booming through my mind: "In order for you to understand suffering, you will need to suffer a great deal. In order for me to teach you, you will get very sick. You will come close to death. For this is the way in our culture."

I replied, "Two of my patients died and I recently had to put my dog down. I am in the South African army and there is apartheid. There is already too much suffering around me and I am only eighteen years old. My life is already over unless I can understand suffering. Please teach me!"

There was a moment's pause and then he showed me visions: the lives of three of my friends and the pain they were in and what they would endure in the future.

Within five years, all of these visions came to pass.

When I awoke, my legs were covered in boils. Despite my shock at seeing the sores, I was exhilarated because I knew the witch doctor had decided to train me. I soon developed piercing headaches and nausea. When I returned to my nursing shift in the army, I was diagnosed with tick-bite fever.

I had been given one answer to the Zen riddle "What is suffering?" And I knew in my bones that I had received my calling to become a sangoma, a traditional South African shaman. I felt blessed by the ancient spirit of Africa, and I knew I had started on a journey filled with magic and danger.

One of the toughest challenges I faced, then and afterward, was my inability to talk to people about these experiences. I was a middle-class white guy in South Africa. Most of my family, friends, and extended community in Johannesburg had no experience with or appreciation of prophetic dreams, and I was concerned how they might respond if I spoke about my calling. Apartheid was still very much in place. I knew I needed to find a flesh-and-blood teacher in this African tradition, but whites were not allowed into the townships (areas reserved exclusively for black people). If I went there I would be questioned by the police and the army—and possibly arrested.

## THE THWASA: THE CALLING ILLNESS

I began to notice changes in my body, mind, and spirit. I became a lot more sensitive. All my senses—especially hearing—were heightened, like those of a leopard. I annoyed my father on numerous occasions by asking him to turn down the TV, despite being on the other side of the house. Birdsong became deeply moving and meaningful, and my love of birds grew; I found solace in the serenading of the many feathered creatures that visited our jungle-like garden day and night.

I felt like a live wire humming with electricity and struggled to sleep at night. I heard the murmurs of ancient African voices. I felt presences descending and teaching me things beyond words and comprehension. I had visions of wild African animals—elephants, lions, leopards, and snakes. Then the visions changed, and my nightly journeys became a space where time fell away and I connected to what prophets call "the timelessness of all things." I felt infinite sadness and suffering, but also boundless joy and abundance. I occasionally woke up feeling like a king with immeasurable riches. My life's purpose was becoming apparent. Old family stories entwined together and connected with my life in an intricate web of truth, mystery, and realization.

The only person I could really talk to about my dreams was my Irish mother. Her mother, my grandmother Mammy Kelly, was well known for her prophetic dreams. They were so strong and accurate that her frightened family begged her to stop sharing them.

I drew African masks with fire inside them. I had a fascination with the eyes, and I often drew flames in their place. The masks could appear grotesque, bizarre, or uplifting, depending on the viewer's perception. They were a way for me to process the nighttime faces and voices that appeared to me in myriad forms.

I felt that some black people could sense what was happening with me, without a word said. One day I was walking to nearby shops after a difficult night of dreams. I knew I looked worn out and haggard. When I walked past a group of black women sitting under a tree talking among themselves, they all stopped talking and stared at me. I saw both compassion and shock in their faces, and I felt instinctively that they had really seen me, my inner being, my soul, and understood that I was going through the thwasa—the calling illness.

The thwasa is found in Southern Africa and among other traditional cultures such as the Siberian peoples in Russia. In fact, it appears in ancient shamanic cultures all over the world. This mystical illness is often preceded by a dream in which ancestors or spirits call the individual for training. It starts to abate once the apprentice finds a teacher.

In the sangoma culture, medicine people are called to become sangomas as I was: through their dreams and the thwasa, which can be very painful physically as well as emotionally, spiritually, and psychologically. It is a delicate process, hardwiring the body, mind, and soul of the initiate to become a "lightning conductor." The thwasa is often misdiagnosed as a psychosomatic illness, but it is much more than that. Its symptoms can include a high temperature, stomach cramps, back pain, weight loss, insomnia, night sweats, lowered immune system, nightmares, anxiety, and depression, to name but a few. I experienced all these symptoms and more over a period of about seven years until I found my teacher.

A key aspect of the illness is an increased psychic awareness or intuition where the initiate learns from the spirit world about other people, animals, or events. Illness and the suffering it brings teach us how to become more human. My own physical pain taught me about humility, surrender, and the importance of prayer.

After recuperating to some degree, I decided to start the university course I had planned to undertake after my army service. I was still feeling weak and unwell, but I was determined to study psychology and hoped I could learn more about my calling illness and find some relief. As part of my psychology training, I also went for traditional psychotherapy sessions and spoke to a few senior psychologists and lecturers at my university about my dreams. I took an interest in Jungian psychology and read most of Carl Jung's works. I loved his writing, but he said nothing that related to my calling illness. I talked with psychologists about my dreams, but this only left me feeling tired and drained. It was an exercise in words rather than understanding; they analyzed my dreams rather than appreciating their sacredness.

One night I dreamed I was in a dentist's chair and one of the psychologists I was confiding in was probing my mouth. When I woke up it was clear to me that analyzing my dreams was not the way to go, so I decided to work with them on my own instead.

My thwasa symptoms continued: chronic exhaustion, nausea, and extreme weight loss coupled with hypersensitivity, sleeplessness, vivid dreams, and nightmares. My immune system was compromised, so I suffered from a number of viral infections. Over a two-year period, I had tick-bite fever twice, glandular fever, bilharzia, and several operations. Yet as my body grew weaker, my psychic abilities grew stronger. That was how I knew this was no ordinary illness or bout of bad health.

At the height of my illness I received a number of dreams about other people, learning things I wouldn't have known in ordinary circumstances. I wasn't sure why this was happening. I could understand dreaming about loved ones such as family and friends, but dreaming about strangers and mere acquaintances was a mystery. It only made sense years later, when I became a diviner and the spirits showed me the intricate pattern of people's lives and where they were struggling; I had to feel their pain in order to help them. The suffering of my thwasa years opened me up to the suffering of the world and prepared me to become an empath.

My nightly journeys picked up momentum. The focus of my calling was on healing, so it made sense that I would dream about other people and their struggles and pain. In one dream, I came across a friend who seemed sad and forlorn and told me he had just broken up with his girlfriend. When I woke up I contacted him, and he told me that he and his girlfriend had indeed parted ways.

No matter how much food I ate, I continued to lose weight. I went for blood tests and spent the night in a top hospital in Johannesburg, where I was examined by specialists. They could find nothing wrong with me. My hands shook as if I'd had ten cups of coffee, and my body was overloaded with energy. Sometimes my hands got incredibly hot. When this happened at home, I placed my hands on my dogs, especially on parts of their body where they were experiencing pain. I found it eased their pain, as well as relieved the excessive heat that was moving through my hands. Once when my dog Sheba was in obvious pain, walking with difficulty and not her usual happy-go-lucky self, I placed my hands on her for ten minutes or so, feeling the heat drain from them. She stayed very still and calm, then wagged her tail and licked me and ran off with a spring in her step. I took this as a sign that the heat and energy in my hands and body had healing properties. And as the heat and charge in my body dissipated, I felt calmer and more grounded.

One day I was having tea with my mother and, as I looked above her head, I felt something shining around her. A voice, a whisper in the wind, told me she would be tested a great deal very soon. I wasn't sure if it was my imagination or not, and I went out for a few hours. But then I felt a strong compulsion to come home again, where I learned that my mother was in the hospital after breaking her wrist in a fall. When I arrived at the hospital and saw her lying in bed, I felt relieved that nothing worse had happened to her, but the following few months brought her a great deal of pain. She had a compound fracture and needed pins inserted to help the bones knit properly.

One day when I was with her, I found my hands heating up and asked if I could put them on her fracture. I felt incredible heat moving through me as I touched her wrist. Afterward, she felt much better and went to sleep. The doctors said that her hand would never be 100 percent again, that she would be lucky to get 80 percent of her original strength back. But I gave her treatments every day, and each time my hands heated up and then she slept. After three months her wrist was completely healed and the doctors were amazed at her recovery.

During these difficult months of psychic phenomena and hypersensitivity, my only solace was my dreams. They became like a road map showing me the way forward, teaching me where to go for help and how to help myself. When I didn't listen, due to tiredness or fear, the dream messages came in another way. They encouraged me to practice yoga and meditation. I found that various yoga postures, such as the shoulder stand and headstand, helped lessen my thwasa symptoms. I also experienced great relief through meditation. If I didn't do it, I was shown various images, such as my zafu, or Zen meditation cushion, sitting in a sea of stillness. These messages were so clear and direct that they propelled me toward regular Zen practice.

While at university, I helped a friend run a meditation center from her home. We practiced meditation based on the teachings of

Zen Master Seung Sahn, the legendary master from South Korea who brought Zen to the West. Sometimes in my daily meditations, I received visions or whispers in the wind offering guidance or encouragement, often in a woman's voice.

## MEETING MY ZEN MASTER

One day I was told that I should practice meditation every day because I would soon meet my teacher in the form of a Zen master. Within six months of this vision I met Mu Deung Sunim, who later became Zen Master Su Bong. Su Bong was a classical Zen monk from South Korea, half Chinese and half Korean, who had been brought up in the Asian community in Hawaii and was called to study with Seung Sahn. After about six years of study, Seung Sahn gave Su Bong *inka*, a mark of spiritual attainment, and allowed him to run retreats.

Zen Masters Seung Sahn (left) and Su Bong.
PHOTO COURTESY OF KWAN UM SCHOOL OF ZEN

Su Bong was short and chubby with a mischievous but compassionate face. He looked like an archetypical Zen master from ancient times, with intense eyes. He could be stern like a lion but also gentle and infinitely compassionate. I knew at once that he was my teacher, and a sense of calm descended on me—I felt that everything would be okay. I knew I had lots of work to do, but my Zen practice provided me with solidity and groundedness. It became an anchor for my nightly journeys and mushrooming psychic ability. Apartheid had prevented me from finding a traditional sangoma teacher, but I knew that for the time being I needed to devote myself to my Buddhist practice, and that when the time was right, I would return to the sangoma path.

Even as my dream life gained momentum, my physical body grew weaker. I went through one infection after another and found it increasingly difficult to balance my spiritual and academic lives. I received powerful visions during my waking life and strong dreams at night. I felt that something was about to shift for me again, and I was nervous, as each time I experienced a premonition it came to pass. My intuition was telling me to prepare for a life of meditation and retreat, while in "reality" I was preparing for my second-year exams.

When the time came for my finals, I calmly entered the examination hall and sat down. I closed my eyes and meditated briefly, breathing in and out. Then, when it was time to start writing, I opened the examination script—and my mind went blank. I couldn't think in words, only images; words no longer made sense. I tried each of the exam's three questions, but all that came out of me was a short paragraph. *Maybe I'm experiencing some kind of panic or anxiety attack*, I thought. I attempted the questions again. Still, all I could see were images, not words. A whisper in the wind told me that my academic career was over for now and that I had to learn about the world beyond words.

I thought I was going crazy, so I closed my eyes and concentrated on my breathing. Yet each time I approached the questions, the same thing happened: no words, only images. I had never given up on anything in my life, but finally I stood up and walked out of the exam hall and away from my academic career.

Within days, I decided to hitchhike through the countryside to a Tibetan Buddhist meditation center in the Karoo (a semi-desert region of South Africa). Meditating there for a week, I received a number of dreams guiding me toward the next stage of my life. In one dream I was shown a particular Buddhist teacher, Antony Osler, who lived on a nearby farm in the Karoo. Inside his home, I saw sacred writings of Buddhist scripture written above his doorway and a host of people walking past him. A voice told me to contact him and that he would know how to help me. I immediately phoned him (in reality) and he invited me to his farm.

Upon entering his home, I felt goose bumps spread all over my body—it was exactly as I had seen it in the dream. Beautifully carved above the doorway was the Buddhist Heart Sutra.

The Heart Sutra is reputed to be the most famous Buddhist text, pointing toward enlightenment and correct understanding. This gave me confidence; I felt I was in the right place. Antony and his wonderful wife, Margie, invited me to live with them. He had a Zen center on his land, and he encouraged me to practice there and work on his land to help ground me. There, I felt at home, settled, where I needed to be.

I had no idea that within a year I would be in South Korea, head shaved, living in a remote monastery. It would be a long way from the student life I'd left behind.

# PART II

## Zen Training

# 3

# African Zen

W ake up, John, wake up!"
I woke with a start, my heart in my mouth and cold
sweat running over me. Every fiber of my being was alert.
A woman's voice was calling me, gentle but insistent. I sat up and
looked around my simple room. Everything was where it should be: a
cardboard box with some of my belongings and a few bags, a candle
and clock on my bedside table. I could hear the wind outside rushing
across the Karoo. My heart beat strongly in my chest. I waited, in tune
with the world around me.

The voice returned. "It is time to start practicing, John." I looked
at the clock; it was around 6 a.m., early—very early, for me. I stood
up, stretched, and got dressed. I walked outside into an icy but
invigorating wind.

As I approached the meditation room, I felt the importance of listening to my dreams and visions. I had no idea where they were leading
me, but I intuitively felt an inner golden thread revealing itself. For my
intuition to work effectively, I had to learn to clear my mind and focus
on the moment. Yet I was overwhelmed with anxiety, a result of the
thwasa, making me supersensitive to everything around me. My senses
were so acute, it sometimes felt as if the universe was crushing down on
my skull. As the thwasa swept through me, meditation was my medicine, giving me the tools to create a sense of spaciousness in my spirit,
a place that held calm, hope, and endless possibilities.

The woman's voice was still with me, radiating through my soul like
an ancient drumbeat calling me to practice and focus my mind. I felt

such magic and wonder, as if I had connected with something sublime and infinitely beautiful.

The zendo, or Zen meditation room, was made from rock. It had once been a goat shed; Antony had renovated it into a beautiful *kerkie*, or church, that seemed to merge with the nearby mountain. As I entered, I knocked myself nearly senseless on the doorframe and staggered like a drunk after a good night out. I would need to remember to duck my skinny six-foot-three frame in the future.

I felt like I was entering an old cave. I smelled Japanese incense mixed with desert sand. I took my shoes off and placed a meditation robe over my shoulders. Placed near the incense sticks was a small wooden sign that read KEEP CLEAR MIND. I smiled. I knew I had come home.

I bowed reverently to the Buddha figure on the altar and walked to my cushion nestled against the wall. I again bowed and then sat cross-legged in the half lotus on my cushion. I slowly breathed down to my *hara* (center), below my navel. I felt the rush of vitality in my body, and I asked myself the age-old questions: "What am I? Why do I eat every day? What is my direction or purpose in life?" I was left with the answer: "I don't know." Time slipped, curved, danced. I entered another space.

The following days and weeks rushed by. Every day I meditated for a few hours and then worked on the farm. I watched the inner dance of my mind, like autumn leaves heralding the upcoming cold Karoo winter. The thwasa dragged on. I experienced stomach cramps and wind, my stomach distended like someone suffering from famine. Yet it wasn't my physical body but my mind that I struggled with most. Sometimes it felt as if my dream world and waking life had merged. A simple cup of tea could turn into a two-hour meditation while I watched the birds in the garden. Nature seemed to be speaking to me in multiple ways. As I watched autumn approach, my eyes focused on a few raindrops falling on the dry earth. I noticed a grasshopper being eaten alive by ants. I tried to rescue it, but the ants were relentless and death came swiftly. Nature was teaching me about impermanence.

A few days later, I woke again with a start, the woman of my dream-time calling me. It was first light, and her voice was crystal clear: "Wait for the next image, John!" Again I got dressed and walked to the zendo. I had no idea what this message, so real yet unearthly, meant.

I had a number of dreams each night. Every day became an exercise in interpreting them. Some dreams were clearly teachings. In one of them, a man in a cowboy hat appeared and said, "Don't believe all the dream images!" This was a wonderful teaching, as I was starting to become ungrounded and take my dreams literally. I was dwelling on my dreamtime, and I felt the danger of living in my mind and getting physically weaker.

"Aaaaaaaaah!" One morning several weeks later, I awoke calling out, shaking in a cold sweat, hearing the gentle woman's voice. "John, you will be tested today like never before. Be careful!" I left my room worried and with a sense of impending doom.

After breakfast, Antony's wife, Margie, greeted me with her characteristic warmth and encouraged me to take Gus the sheepdog for a walk. Gus was delightful and mischievous, with a mind of his own, and always seemed to get his nose stuck somewhere he shouldn't.

I dashed off into the Karoo bush following Gus. I still felt apprehensive, but the day was changing. The clouds had parted, it was warmer now, and I could see the first glimmer of sunlight raking the hills in glorious light.

I followed Gus through the bush as he sniffed down holes following a trail. The day was becoming hotter by the minute—the temperature must have been close to one hundred degrees. I rested under a tree and sipped some water. I sensed something ominous, a feeling that only grew as we moved toward a dry riverbed. Maybe I was getting overanxious, obsessed with my own thoughts. But I sensed the presence of death, as if people had been murdered in this place in the past. This feeling was strong, and I couldn't shake it. I felt afraid, and . . . where was Gus?

I shouted for him. I could barely see him in the distance. Everything was so still. I felt hostile presences in the air, spooky and strange. The energy of the ravine spirits seemed to increase, and they magnified the longer I stayed in the ravine. I desperately tried to get away.

Suddenly a scream of pain cut the air like a knife. The hidden presences seemed to come alive. I was petrified—I felt I might die. I followed the sound. About twenty yards ahead I found Gus, caught in a large trap with metal teeth. It had snapped firmly around one of his hind legs. He was bleeding. Mad with pain and fear, he tried to bite me when I approached. I spoke gently to him, but it had no effect. Gus was howling and biting the air.

I tried but couldn't open the trap. It weighed almost as much as Gus. I lifted him and the trap, and I ran. I didn't want Gus to die, not today, not like this.

I tore up the ravine while Gus tried to bite me. Then I stopped and put an old bandage I had retrieved earlier from the farmhouse around his mouth so he couldn't bite me. The hidden presences seemed to be all around me, running after me. Ahead rose a sheer cliff. I heard baboons calling in the distance and felt Gus's feverish panic and an ominous force trying to claim me. So I moved up the cliff, over stones and boulders. It was hard going but I flew as if possessed by a hidden power.

I was halfway up the cliff when my knees felt strange: a warning from my body. I went into overdrive—I didn't want Gus to die. I felt sad, alone, and so fragile. I had seen too much suffering in the army. The death and pain in the soldiers' eyes had burned into my soul. I loved animals. I loved Gus. Today he would live. I was going to do everything in my power to save him. I couldn't save my fellow soldiers or take away their pain. But today, I could at least save this dog's life.

We reached the top and I placed Gus in the shade of a large boulder. I took the bandage off from around his mouth. He was panting furiously but wasn't trying to bite me anymore. I said a small prayer, hoping he would be okay. The farmhouse was a couple of miles away over rough terrain. I told Gus I would soon return, and I ran. I ran for my soldier patients, for their pain and suffering, for my own pain and misunderstood illness. And for Gus.

When I reached the farmhouse, I called out to Margie and told her what had happened. She said there was a simple way to open this kind of trap—a jackal trap. When we returned to Gus, he seemed calm and quiet in the shade of the boulder. Margie took charge, and within a few minutes Gus was free. He was so happy. He went scampering over the rocks on three legs. I was amazed by his agility.

The next morning when I woke up, both my knees had swollen to twice their normal size. I hobbled outside and saw Gus going about his farm duties on three legs. The damaged leg looked better. I suddenly realized—Gus was in much better shape than I was! I recalled the woman's voice the morning before. I sensed that I had passed my test, but clearly not unscathed.

As the wind whistled through the Karoo, my mind restlessly meandered over the day's events. I didn't know why the woman had warned me about the test I endured, and I couldn't understand the fear and panic that had overwhelmed me earlier in the dry ravine as I felt the presence of a force racing after me. Was it my own mind, or had I awoken something else on my simple summer walk? My senses were heightened, and I found that I welcomed the pain in my knees; it helped ground me in the present. I was nervous about how quickly my mind and spirit could soar into the other world filled with forces that were ancient, alive, and unconcerned with the living or the dead.

I was worried about my own mental health. Had I imagined the presences in the dry riverbed? Fortunately, Margie confirmed my intuition, telling me that many years ago during one of the Anglo-Boer wars, men had died in the ravine.

Years later when I shared this story, my sangoma teacher said my ancestral spirits were testing me: When the veil between the living and dead was thin, how would I deal with it? In particular, how would I deal with spirits who were caught between the worlds as a result of violent or traumatic death? With sangoma training, we often receive difficult tests in the beginning to show us where we need to put our attention in order to grow and strengthen. I had received my test, and I spent the next ten years strengthening my spirit.

Sadly, I had to leave the farm to get proper medical attention for my knees. I rested up with my parents in Johannesburg, listening to the wind and watching the birds. I spent my days exercising my knees, watching my dreams, and playing with my dogs. Life was filled with pain—and mystery. My nighttime journeys kept beckoning me to another world where magic was real and infinite possibilities existed, unhampered by earthly boundaries of thoughts or perceptions.

One day while walking in my garden I received a vision. A woman's voice addressed me with utter clarity and authority, cutting through my thoughts of physical pain and loneliness. She said that I needed to devote myself to spiritual practice and learn all I could from my spiritual teachers because one day I would be called on to help the world. I would know it was my time when a wave of water killed a large number of people. It would be the biggest natural disaster in recent time, and it would happen about ten years in the future. She warned me to work hard, for I needed to be ready when I was called.

When the tsunami hit Indonesia more than ten years later, in 2004, I was doing a yoga retreat on an island off the west coast of Ireland. My whole body started shaking, and I felt called to become a spiritual teacher.

We had a happy meditation center in my university town, where I was staying with friends to take part in our upcoming annual retreat. Students and academics came to sit with us twice a week. Often the meetings turned into social events with long tea sessions on the *stoep* (patio) while we watched the sun go down. We tried to ignore the squalor of the township just over the hill while we talked about philosophy, psychology, and mind-expanding activities such as meditation and holotropic breathing. Politics rarely came up because we felt numb and powerless in the face of our totalitarian government and guilty about our privileged lifestyles. It was far easier to intellectualize about life and the beauty in our dreams.

But my dreams were often mingled with nightmares. I felt as if I was fighting in a war each night. In the mornings I would wake up, meditate, and drink tea like the colonialists of old. My daylight hours were dreamlike, and I was often afraid to sleep. The year was 1992 and Nelson Mandela was in the news because he had been invited by the national government for talks. He had been released from prison on Robben Island in February 1990. The light was starting to show in the dark tunnel of our South Africa.

While we drank our tea, we could smell the wood and coal fires of the township folk over the hill. Sometimes I could almost feel the whispers, prayers, hopes, and dreams in the township smoke as I breathed it in. I could taste the poverty of life there, and I felt both lucky and ashamed to be so privileged. I felt the souls of the people crying out in pain, and at night the African ancestors of the living approached me and taught me their ways. I awoke feeling helpless. I didn't know any witch doctors, herbalists, or African healers. How could I begin to understand the mysteries of Africa and my own dreams?

To ease my mind and ground my spirit, I sometimes went surfing with Zane, a good friend of mine. Surfing was a meditation for us, a constant dance between surrendering and using our willpower. Nature was the guiding teacher. With every wave and gust of wind, I found the answers to my prayers and dreams. When I surrendered to the water and the feeling of the waves around me, I felt part of something much greater. I too became a drop of water in the sea.

But then I felt called to surf the waves of my mind instead. I sold my wetsuit and used the proceeds to go on a three-day retreat with Zen Master Su Bong.

Su Bong arrived at the retreat with a flurry of energy, a big smile, and an intensity of purpose. He brought with him a tornado of dharma energy.

If you were in his presence for even a few minutes, you felt compelled to meditate and seek answers to the age-old questions: "What is life?" "Who am I?" Why do I eat every day?" He lived as if every second counted; nothing was wasted and everything was important. He walked his talk. He spoke about the importance of correct action. He gave dharma (spiritual teachings) talks that made us laugh and cry. And he inspired us to meditate as if our very lives depended on it. We often heard him say, "What is your direction? Why are you alive? This is very important. You must find the answer!"

On our retreat we meditated for about four to six hours every day, attended dharma talks, and had private interviews with Su Bong. It was an auspicious weekend for me because I turned twenty-one. In my interview, Su Bong sat across from me on a black cushion. With a beaming smile, he gestured toward me to sit down in front of him. I thought he must have had some good dreams the night before.

I thought my cushion was too close to him. I felt nervous, overwhelmed by his tornado energy. I started to pull the cushion away. Suddenly he shouted at me and poked me in the stomach with his Zen stick. "Hey, not so far back! I need you close to me so I can hit you with my stick if I need to!" Then he roared with laughter in his mischievous, boyish way.

I looked at his stick. It was about three to four feet long, made from hardwood, beautifully gnarled and well-polished—a sight to behold, just like its owner.

"What is universal sound?" he shouted at me. My mind went blank. He had already given us a few talks about Zen *kong-ans*, or riddles, used for centuries by Zen masters to steer students into the present moment, encouraging them to go beyond rational thinking and the dualism of the mind—to see clearly, feel clearly, and then walk and talk clearly.

I started to speak. Zen Master Su Bong shouted at me again. "No words, John! Demonstrate!" So I hit the ground with my hand. He smiled and poked me in the belly with his stick. "Correct! But you are a big man—hit the ground properly." Again he asked me, "What is universal sound?" I replied by hitting the ground hard with my hand while staring at him, taking in his energy, smile, funny clothes, and stick. He laughed and exclaimed, "Wonderful!" He then asked me, "Why do you eat every day?"

I replied, "I don't know."

"What is your direction?" (Meaning what was my calling, or life path.)

I again replied, "I don't know!"

He smiled at me, his head glistened, and he picked up his stick and rested against it, grinning. "Okay, but you must find the answer! Practice hard, breathing in 'What am I?' breathing out 'Don't know.' Then one day helping sentient beings will be possible." Su Bong brought his hands together and bowed to me. I responded by bowing to him. The interview was over. I walked toward the door. As I touched the door knob, Su Bong shouted at me, "You are not special! None of us are! I am just doing Zen Master job, and you are just doing student job. Okay?"

"Yes, sir!" I replied. I bowed again and left the interview room.

*You are not special!* became like a mantra banging away in my mind.

I guess I had thought I was quite special. I had nice flowing blond hair tied back by a colorful bandanna, and I was tall and skinny in an elfin way. Yet the more I thought of his words, the more peace I felt. Being special brings a sense of responsibility, the need to be better than others. His words unleashed a spirit of equanimity. I felt deflated but also humbled and grounded in a way I had not felt before. The world seemed to open before me.

After one memorable meditation session, Su Bong lifted his stick in the air, pointed in the direction of the township over the hill, and brought his stick down onto the ground with a crescendo of sound and energy, waking every one of us. Then he shouted with extraordinary ferocity and strength, "Some kind of demonstration is needed!" I took him to mean a demonstration to help heal the injustice of the squalor in the townships. The whole room shook with his outburst, leaving a stony silence in its wake. We were all white middle-class students or academics, and there was a sense of hidden shame and guilt in the room. We immediately looked to one of our meditation elders, Antony, who was also an accomplished human rights lawyer, as if to say, "Here is one of us who is doing something!" But that was not enough. We felt helpless and angry with Su Bong for his apparent judgment of us. What could we do? How could we heal our country?

During one of our private exchanges during the retreat, I told Su Bong I had dropped out of university because of ill health. He looked at me with compassion in his eyes and said, "You must finish school!" I described to him what had happened there and how words had lost meaning for me, and he sat for a moment and reflected. He said I had made some progress along the Zen road of transformation; I had attained a stage of the journey, namely, that emptiness is form and form is emptiness. He felt that I understood some important truths, but the journey had only begun.

In Zen they say when you start the journey of "What am I?" mountains are mountains and rivers are rivers. After hard practice, mountains are no longer mountains and rivers are no longer rivers. Your way of seeing the world changes. That was the place I was in. In order for me to see the world as it was again, I would need to practice very hard.

Toward the end of the retreat, I took my five precepts—a mark of commitment to Buddhist practice under a particular teacher and dharma lineage—with Zen Master Su Bong. In the Korean lineage, the practitioner is burned with a stick of incense. The sharp sting of the burn is said to represent the burning of past karma and the beginning of a new life. Each precept ceremony ends with the students being given new names to highlight their destiny or what they are trying to achieve in their lives. The name I was given was Hae Jok, meaning "wisdom stillness." *Hae*, wisdom, was the "family" name of our group of practitioners who were taking the precepts together. *Jok*, stillness, was my personal name. This felt very apt, as stillness was what I was aiming to achieve with my practice.

In the lead-up to our precepts ceremony, I had a very successful interview with Su Bong. I had been working on a particular kong-an for some time, and I managed to answer it correctly. I felt light, ecstatic, and free. I hardly felt my feet as I bounced up off my Zen cushion.

Then Su Bong asked me another riddle. I had no answer, and so the journey continued.

I discussed with Su Bong the possibility of enrolling in his three-month retreat, called *Kyol Che* (tight fist), in South Korea, where numerous hours are spent in meditation, chanting, and bowing. I asked his permission, and he agreed. I was elated. There were gentle murmurs inside my mind during meditation about becoming a monk, and I thought this experience would help me decide. I would join Su Bong for the winter Kyol Che starting in November 1993 in a temple called Hwa Gye Sa, in the mountains just outside Seoul.

Two important events transpired to catapult me into the ancient world of Korean Zen. The first was illness. I contracted hepatitis A, a debilitating condition that affects the liver. I lost even more weight and my skin turned an orangey yellow color. At certain points I became delirious, and when I slept I felt like I had entered the spirit world. On waking each morning my body felt heavy. I felt nauseous most of the time, and it was difficult to eat. My mind lingered on death and the thought that maybe it was better than the life I was leading. South Korea and the possibilities it offered me seemed far away, a distant dream. Doubts entered my mind. I sat listlessly on my Zen cushion during the day and then pulled myself up for bed. The thought kept occurring to me, *How can I possibly go to South Korea in a few months when I am so sick now?*

Then I dreamed I was riding an elephant on a mountain in the Far East and was surrounded by monks who were also riding elephants. A voice said to me, "Do not under any circumstances cancel your trip to Korea! It is an important part of your journey and holds the key to your destiny." I woke startled. I could still feel the mountain breeze, the monks, and the elephants.

My father was very worried about my safety amid the tensions between North and South Korea. Their saber rattling appeared ominous, and the world was uncertain as to whether it would result in serious conflict and possibly war. He insisted I first meet with the

South Korean ambassador. Only if this official told me it was safe to travel there could I go.

I met the ambassador with a friend of mine. The ambassador was a friendly man with passable English, but he kept a dictionary in his lap while my friend and I spoke to him. My friend was rather impatient and kept finishing his sentences for him.

The ambassador said, "So the situation between North and South is—"

"Fine, everything is fine, isn't it?" my friend interrupted.

The ambassador replied, "Ah, yes, fine, fine . . ." as he ran his finger slowly down the list of words in his dictionary. This continued for a few minutes until he walked over to us with a big smile and shook our hands, saying, "Enjoy Korea. It beautiful country, it is."

I thought, *I'm sure it is.*

When I returned home, there was a fax waiting for me from Zen Master Seung Sahn in South Korea. It read, "Everything good in South Korea. Any more questions ask the sky?" I appreciated this zany logic. Now the prospect of going to Korea was exciting beyond words.

When the time to travel there arrived at last, my skin was no longer yellow and my hepatitis had healed sufficiently for travel. Because my knees were still not strong, Zen Master Su Bong had given me special permission to meditate in a chair. I was now on my way to the mountain kingdom of South Korea.

# 4

# South Korea

After almost twenty-three hours of traveling from South Africa, my mind was a daze of colors, sights, and sounds. I was now riding in a taxi with a monk friend. Inside our taxi all was still as my friend fingered his prayer beads and the world outside passed by. The fragrance of incense and the sounds of chanting wafted toward us as we approached the temple. People dashed to and fro. Motorbikes and scooters dodged pedestrians on the sidewalks. Monks in gray robes walked calmly among the chaos.

Hwa Gye Sa temple was over six hundred years old and now the home of Zen Master Su Bong and Grand Master Seung Sahn (Zen Master of my Zen Master). I spent my first night there in a small monk's room, seven by five feet. It was cold outside, and the under-floor heating was turned up high. The sound of water rustling through the water pipes below me mingled with the chanting monks above and the smell of strong incense as I drifted off to sleep.

*"Kwan Se-um Bo-sal, Kwan Se-um Bo-sal, Kwan Se-um Bo-sal . . ."* Chanting from the temple above woke me in the early morning, sounding like a hive of bees calling on me to wake up on a deeper level. My essential nature, bones, blood, and DNA were all being called to wake up. It was just after 6 a.m. and morning practice had begun. I got dressed and walked to the Zen center at the top of the temple. We were making

history—this was the first time monks, nuns, laypeople, and Westerners from a host of countries would be practicing together for the duration of winter Kyol Che. It was exciting to feel the temple moving to the sound of ancient bells and social change.

After being in the temple for a few days on a hilltop overlooking Seoul, I left to explore the city. I passed a large girls' school. I was only aware of it on my return journey, when I was jolted to my senses by the sounds of whistling and screaming. I turned to see girls hanging out the window and shouting at me mischievously. I checked to make sure I was dressed properly and didn't have my fly undone, and then looked up and down the road to see if they were whistling at someone else. I kept thinking that if this was a preliminary initiation to becoming a monk, my life was about to become very interesting. Apparently, they had never seen a blond Westerner before.

But my pop star days were short-lived; we were about to have our heads shaved in preparation for Kyol Che. I took this in stride, having gone through a similar experience in the army, though this time I would be completely bald.

Getting my head shaved was exhilarating! It was a joyful ceremony filled with laughter. As each tuft of hair fell to the ground, I felt lighter and lighter. By the end I was giddy, elated, as if I had taken a magic elixir. It was like witnessing my old life and saying good-bye to it with humor and fun—a good way to start a new chapter in my life.

Before the retreat started, I asked for a private audience with Grand Master Seung Sahn Soen-sa, known by his students as Dae Soen Sa Nim, the head of our lineage and guiding teacher of Hwa Gye Sa. In the Korean tradition, all Zen masters are referred to as "Soen Sa Nim." "Dae" (great) is added to their title when a teacher turns sixty. He was surrounded with myths and legends, and was known as the "magic Zen master" or "shaman Zen master" because he had obtained enlightenment at the tender age of twenty-two. There were many tales of his feats of magic. For instance, one day the monks said he shook the whole monastery by clanging pots and pans, waking everyone up. When they went outside, they found him standing on top of a flagpole. They had no idea how he got up there.

Another story was that he used to wake up between midnight and 3 a.m. for "special energy" practice in his American Zen centers, waking his students with strange sounds and shouting emanating from his room. When his monks inquired about all the noise, he said he was fighting off demons that were trying to prevent the next age of enlightenment among mankind.

Shaking with nervousness about this meeting, I took off my shoes and entered Dae Soen Sa Nim's room. He was sitting cross-legged on a cushion on the floor. A few monks were serving him and asking him questions. I was asked to sit in front of him on a cushion. He gave me a big smile, and I bowed reverently in return, which is customary. He pointed for me to sit down and then said in a booming voice, "Any questions?" He was a busy man and liked to get straight to the heart of the matter. He was used to his Western students asking many questions, after which he would laugh and ask a few of his own, leaving everyone stupefied and in profound reflection. This was his job, and he did it very well.

In my mind I had rehearsed my speech a thousand times. I thought about telling him about my dreams and experiences, the pain of apartheid South Africa, and the suffering of soldiers in the South African army. Yet in the moment with him, all thoughts seemed to narrow and solidify into one piercing question.

"How can I help people?" I asked him, my voice hoarse.

Much to my surprise, Dae Soen Sa Nim burst out laughing and then mimicked me. "How can I help people?" he squealed in a high voice. He then turned to his monks and did the same thing. The whole room was in an uproar of laughter. Then his voice and face changed to stone and he looked directly at me, pointed at my stomach with his stick, and shouted, "You have no center—how can you help this world? First, you must develop a strong center. Then helping this world is possible. Okay?"

I replied, "Okay!"

He said, "You are crazy. You have to become 100 percent crazy. Then helping this world is possible." He paused a moment as he looked deeply at me. "You have monk's face! What is your practice?"

I mentioned the mantra practice that Su Bong gave me.

"Goooood! Zen Master Su Bong is number one good Zen master. So only breathe in and breathe out. Then only 'What am I? Don't know!' Then saving this world is possible. Okay?"

"Okay, sir," I said, "Thank you, sir."

"No problem. So you are doing Kyol Che. That is wonderful. So practice very hard, get enlightenment, and save this world from suffering. Okay?"

"Okay, sir, I will do my best."

"Don't do your best, just do it, okay!?" he bellowed.

"Okay, sir!" I said. I bowed reverently to him and slowly walked outside into a beautiful autumn day.

Each day came and went without much change until the retreat entered its second month. We meditated like soldiers searching for clarity of mind while we plumbed the depths of our souls. The snow had come, and everything was white and beautiful. Some of us were starting to go crazy from the routine of no talking, long hours of meditation, and not enough sleep. We were like soda bottles that had been shaken too much, waiting to explode in foam and bubbles.

One night after final practice at 9 p.m., Su Bong asked us to help him perform a "bodhisattva action" and sweep the temple grounds after a recent snowfall. (Bodhisattvas are people devoted to releasing sentient beings from suffering.) He was worried about the ice in the early hours when the old people arrived at the temple for practice.

The snow was deep and powdery. We were all exhausted, but we willingly followed our Zen master and methodically swept the temple steps. The wind had just stopped, and the sound of raking snow and padded feet filled the air. I was almost at the highest of a series of temples and was raking from side to side when I noticed a hurricane of snow and wind in front of me and a voice saying, "Sweep downward!" I smiled. It was Zen Master Su Bong, leading by example.

Dae Soen Sa Nim had given us a series of dharma talks (teachings) based on his recent book, *The Compass of Zen*. These talks were filled with humor, laughter, and serious reflections. He believed that human beings had lost their way and that the overpopulation of the world could be attributed to the millions of animals who were killed over the two previous centuries, referring to the widespread killing of horses and buffalo in America. He told us cause and effect was very clear: these animals became humans in their next life—humans who have animal consciousness. It was still possible for them to become enlightened, but more difficult than if they had human consciousness. Animal consciousness meant they mainly thought about sex, food, and basic survival needs. It was vital for human beings to find their direction, and meditation practice focusing on self-inquiry and mindfulness would help this process.

We were encouraged to go beyond what we could see and perceive with our senses, to penetrate the world beyond form. Opposites were a core theme in our Zen talks. Sometimes Dae Soen Sa Nim mentioned South Africa and California in the same sentence. He said, "South Africa number one bad situation, but very good for spiritual practice. California number one good situation, but very difficult for spiritual practice." Some of us had come from countries experiencing profound social change and disruption, such as eastern Europe and South Africa. A few of the laymen had been soldiers in Russia and Poland. We practiced like our very lives depended on it. We were in great pain, and our people, including our governments and politicians, had no answers for us. Dae Soen Sa Nim felt that if people had it easy like they did in California, it would be harder to delve deeper into the roots of suffering and the human condition.

During these morning talks, Dae Soen Sa Nim always asked people if they had any questions. Then he would chuckle gently and laugh hysterically, eliciting openness in all of us. "Any kind of question is okay," he would say. Slowly but surely, people raised their hands one by one.

One person asked, "Is there life on other planets? Are we alone in the universe?"

Dae Soen Sa Nim responded with another question: "Do you think that human beings are special? Of course there is life out there. If we think of the universe like the human body, planet Earth is just one small bump on this body. Okay?"

He finished with great laughter, and we all responded together—"Okay!"

These talks always filled us with humor, lightness, and a profound emptiness and sense of the unknown. We entered the world of the mystic, the world of "Don't know." "What am I? Don't know. What is this? Don't know. Why do we eat every day? Don't know." Everything was open, and the circle of Zen beckoned to us all.

Around two months in, my body was starting to heal. I felt clearer and stronger than I had for the last four years. But I had succumbed to a strange fever, and my voice had completely gone. My throat swelled and I could feel a bump on one side of it. The monks took me to see Dae Soen Sa Nim's Chinese doctor, revered throughout Korea. He examined me thoroughly and gave me an elixir of strong Chinese medicine to drink during the day. It was black, and it smelled awful and tasted very bitter, like drinking an oak tree. My monk friends told me that the bitter taste was a good sign and an indication of the potency of the medicine, so I diligently drank it.

I also saw Dr. Lee, a well-known Chinese acupuncturist who meditated with us and had made it known that he would help the monks and fellow retreatants if they needed him. He was so proficient with the needles that I hardly felt them penetrate my skin, and the needles worked on every level. I felt wonderful afterward and looked forward to more meditation.

We had a week of intense practice during our retreat that involved Zen interviews every day and practice until midnight. We had only three hours of sleep per night. The idea behind this was to elevate our self-inquiry and plunge us into the world of "What am I?" Hopefully, something would open inside us like a lotus flower.

Every day, I walked downstairs for my interview with Master Su Bong. One day I entered the interview in a rush and threw my scarf and hat in the corner. Su Bong barked at me, saying, "Everything is part of you. That scarf and hat are protecting and serving you! Treat them accordingly!" I gently picked them up, folded them, and carefully placed them beside me. He smiled and said, "Correct!" We then proceeded with the interview.

Su Bong asked me a few kong-ans. These Zen riddles put you in a state of existential angst, and the only way to answer them is to meditate and surrender to the moment: surrender to knowing the answer—and to not knowing. I was told, "Meditate like a cat watching a mouse hole, vigilant, alert, and prepared to strike!" Zen riddles always focus on the here and now.

Su Bong once asked me, "How can you help South Africa, John? Is Mandela right or wrong?"

As I started to answer, he smiled and held up his hand and said, "Go beyond your opinions. You are almost there, John, just one more step. Many people have attained enlightenment in our school, John. Just one more step, okay?"

"Okay, sir," I said. I bowed reverently and left the room.

Then one day I noticed a change in Su Bong—subtle but powerful. A gray pallor had descended upon him, like an aura. He became more serious in his teachings. He still made us laugh, but his teachings had a somber edge to them, as if to say, "This is it. We are living close to the edge. The world as we know it is changing, and possibly fading."

One night after evening practice, he gave a dharma talk. He looked to me like a piece of granite carved out of a mountain. He paused, held his Zen stick firmly, and said, "There are many worlds within this world. There are demons and there are angels. There is everything in this world. Everything is alive, everything is real. What are you going to follow? What are you going to believe in?"

The tone and energy of his words left us all speechless, and I went to bed with his words ringing in my sleep. I heard his voice telling me I was almost there, just one more step. Did that mean I should become a Zen monk in South Korea? I wasn't sure. With only three hours a night to sleep, I was so tired. I did some Zen energy exercises. The wind picked up outside, and I heard the temple chimes ringing loudly to the rhythm of the winter snow.

The retreat came and went like the passing seasons. At certain times it felt so long, and I wondered if it would ever end. But the days moved like the wind, and as the snow melted outside, the retreat drew to a close. I was in a state of confusion when the last ceremony closed. Should I become a Zen monk and stay here? I still felt the thwasa illness inside of me and the call of the sangoma, but now it was a whisper. I felt at home and accepted in the temple like never before.

I had become friends with a few senior monks and shared my confusion about whether to become a monk and join them full time in the temple. I asked Mu Sang Sunim, one of the senior monks, to discuss my situation with Zen Master Seung Sahn—I was too nervous to approach him again. It is said that Kyol Che is like flying; the takeoff is relatively easy but the landing can take some time.

The monks were going to Singapore to assist Su Bong in opening a Chinese Zen temple. I accompanied them to have more time with my teachers and help me make my decision. At one point during the temple opening festivities, I was ushered into a car with Su Bong Soen-sa on my right and Dae Soen Sa Nim on my left. I felt as if I was surrounded by two powerful balls of energy. They both took out their mala (prayer) beads and did their practice. The driver drove and the Zen masters meditated in silence. I froze, breathed, froze, and meditated as well. What else was there to do in that moment?

I had another interview with Su Bong. Right before it, a female voice told me, gently but seriously, "This will be your final interview with Su Bong in this life. Don't worry—it will be okay." I shook inside hearing this, yet our interview went well. Su Bong smiled lovingly at me. I seemed to have made progress over the last three months. Again he said to me, "Just one more step, John, you are almost there!"

As I left the interview room, I felt confused and very sad, my premonition echoing in my mind. I passed by a Chinese monk and then picked up a magazine with Su Bong on the cover. I started to draw on his face with a black pen, absentmindedly blackening out his mouth. Seeing this, the monk shouted at me in English, "Hey, man, why you draw on your teacher's face?"

I was shocked—this woke me up. I didn't know why I had done that.

Our beloved Zen masters were on their way to Hong Kong to assist our Zen community and lead more retreats. I went with them to the airport. Dae Soen Sa Nim smiled at me and asked me to sit beside him. I was petrified, as he had huge energy, and my body shook in his presence. He was very direct, saying, "I spoke to Mu Sang Sunim. He told me about your confusion. Confusion not necessary. You join my monk army, okay?"

I stumbled and tried to speak. He slapped my leg—hard. "Just do it, okay?"

"I'm only twenty-two years old," I explained.

He felt my hesitation. "Twenty-two no problem. I got enlightenment at twenty-two. Join my monk army, then save all beings from suffering."

My voice was in my throat. His energy was taking me to my edge. I was being forced to make a decision, to find my direction. And I did.

Everything became crystal clear. I realized in that moment that I needed to return to South Africa, vote for Mandela, and find a sangoma teacher. My job was to become an African monk, a sangoma.

"I can't!" I told Zen Master Seung Sahn.

I returned to South Africa and reenrolled at my old university to finish my studies. I knew Su Bong would be happy about this. He always wanted me to finish my studies. I voted for Mandela, and Mandela became president. It was now 1994 and South Africa had ushered in a new phase of democracy and equality for all people. I felt happy and quietly confident that I would find a sangoma teacher.

The months passed quickly. There was a whisper in the wind, and one night I had nightmares. I saw Su Bong with a gray face. He kept telling me not to worry. Still, I worried.

After breakfast one morning I received a phone call: Su Bong had died in the Hong Kong Zen Center the way he lived. He was giving a Zen interview to a young girl and asked her, "What is universal consciousness?"

She responded, and he said, "Correct!" He remained sitting upright while his head fell forward and he died of a massive heart attack.

His death was devastating to me and our small Buddhist community in South Africa. Yet although his body was gone, his teachings have never left me, and his voice continues to ring through my mind at important times in my life.

# PART III

Dreaming of Leopards and Dancing
with Spirits—The Sangoma Way

# 5

# My Teacher Appears

In 1995 I returned to university in South Africa to finish my degree in psychology. Part of my training involved helping a professor with an AIDS-awareness campaign in the high schools of our local township—a unique opportunity for me to gain access to the townships, which would have been nearly impossible without the official backing of a university program. Although South Africa was now a democratic country, fear and distrust between whites and blacks remained widespread.

The professor believed that to help the local community, we needed to understand the traditional African ways of healing illness, so he arranged for us to talk to Mkhuseli, a well-known herbalist in the township. About twenty of us gathered in a small room under a corrugated iron roof. The herbalist, a mature man in his fifties, talked with conviction and authority. He spoke in his native language, isiXhosa. Our interpreter, Thandisizwe, was also Xhosa, with a wonderful eloquence and grasp of the English language. (Xhosa is pronounced KOH-sah, with a click in the "Xh" part of the word, like the click you make in your throat when you call a horse.)

The professor asked Mkhuseli how herbalists and other traditional healers go about healing people with severe illnesses. Mkhuseli told us about the river people, the *abantu bomlambo*, and how important it is to connect with these ancestors below the waters. He said healers make an offering of tobacco and prayers to a still pond, river, or lake. If the abantu bomlambo accept the prayers, an invisible hand will reach up and bring the tobacco to the bosom of the river people, who will then bestow healing and blessings to the people above.

At this point the professor interrupted Mkhuseli and ended the conversation, thanking him for his time but saying it was lunchtime and we had to go. While our professor had been eager to expose us to African traditional ways, their mystical approach had apparently left him dumbstruck and confused.

Weeks later when I asked the professor if we could invite herbalists from the township to lecture in the classroom, he said, "But why, John? We are the dominant culture!"

In a way, his rejection was a gift. I finally understood what was calling me to the very heart of nature and being, and the conflict between the modern, Western, and secular world and the traditional, spiritual, African approach. I knew in my heart that I had to make peace with my own dreams and listen to the ancient voice inside me, a voice that my modern Western mentors and guides would not hear. I had to be brave and take a leap of faith.

In those days I didn't yet understand the isiXhosa language, but my body wisdom and spirit knew what Mkhuseli was saying. After the professor abruptly interrupted him "for lunch," a surge of anger spurred me to start my own personal Xhosa journey. I turned to Thandisizwe with full conviction and said, "Thandisizwe, please take me to see a sangoma. I want a divination session. I want someone who is good and honest. I don't want a tourist experience. Please take me to someone you yourself would go to."

Thandisizwe told me his young son had just been sick and his wife had taken him to a sangoma woman. She was honest, straight talking, and very strong, and she had helped his son get better. We would go to see her the next day.

That night my teacher-to-be had a dream. The Great Spirit, uThixo, appeared and told her to be prepared because someone from another culture would soon come to her and she would train him to become a senior sangoma like herself.

The next day I met MaMngwevu for the first time. As Thandisizwe and I entered her home, she was sweeping her yard and hanging clothes on the fence. She had an aura of strength about her and appeared quite stern. Thandisizwe greeted her in a friendly way, and she gestured toward her divination room.

The small room was made from mud and cow dung, very neat and orderly inside, with a peach-pink wash on the walls. A strong smell of herbs lingered in the air. Animal pelts were draped on the walls, and simple implements such as a grate and a large flat stone used for crushing herbs lay on the floor. I felt transported to the time before white people came to this part of the Eastern Cape.

My first divination session was a remarkable event. My past, present, and future melted together in a session that seemed to last for hours. It was as though I had physically entered the dream world, and my physical reality and dreams became one.

MaMngwevu beckoned us to sit in front of her on a mat on the ground with our feet facing her, hands and legs uncrossed. She sat on a small wooden stool with a towel neatly draped across her legs. She wore white clay around her eyes, a wonderful array of beads around her forehead, and white beads around her neck. A colorful towel wound like a turban on her head. She appeared stately and noble, with a powerful spirit, and I was drawn to her beautiful, finely shaped hands. I felt the ancient world flooding through her eyes; they were kind, with all the suffering of the world in them and without judgment.

She said a few words to us about the money for the divination, which we folded under the mat. There was a moment—a pause, like the still point in the eye of a hurricane—and we all breathed in together. Then Mama began to talk. Her voice was loud, changing in pitch, and her body shook. She was speaking deep, old isiXhosa, and the resonant clicks filled the small mud hut. "*Camgawini bahlakasi bam*" (I honor and praise the ancestors, the revered ones), she said.

I felt hot inside and my body trembled. My ears rang to the sound of MaMngwevu's shouts. It felt like her words were whipping my spirit back to life.

There was a rhythm to her divination, like the sea moving in and out. Each time she paused and made a point, Thandisizwe responded with, "*Camagu mhlekazi.*" (I honor and respect you, revered Mother.) I followed suit. "Camagu mhlekazi."

I didn't know isiXhosa, but my soul knew what she was saying. I knew the witch doctor from my dreams was beckoning me to follow in this ancient African way. MaMngwevu pointed to me as her voice reached a fever pitch, and the whole hut seemed to shake. I knew this was the turning point—and I was afraid.

Thandisizwe translated quickly: MaMngwevu could see that I had the calling illness, the thwasa, and that I had been sick for a very long time. She went into details about my illness: the pain in my legs, my low energy and fatigue, the fact that sometimes I just wanted to die. She said I had been called by the river and sea people, and had almost gone to them. It was true; I had been swept out to sea three times, and very nearly lost my life in the treacherous waters off the Eastern Cape.

MaMngwevu spoke in detail about my life over the past seven years and how alone and lost I had felt. She mentioned my inner world and that I liked to be on my own, away from people. This was also true—I felt drawn to the natural world, the world beyond words, and alienated from my white middle-class background and the people who didn't seem to understand me. She knew that my knees were very weak from my climbing mishap in the Karoo with Gus and a more recent injury in the sea in Zululand.

She had tears in her eyes as she spoke. She seemed to really know me, to know my spirit.

There was another pause, between Thandisizwe translating and MaMngwevu's talking, and we filled it with "*Siyavuma!*" (We agree.) Then MaMngwevu and I simply looked at each other.

"*Kutheni uthathe ixesha elide kangaka ukuza apha?*" (What took you so long to come to me?) she asked.

I replied, "Apartheid, Mama."

Her eyes glistening with tears, she said, *"Ahh, Thixo, Nkosi yam, siphantse saphulukana nawe!"* (Oh Lord, my God, we almost lost you!)

Then she told me her dream and said I was the one she was to train.

There were tears in my eyes too. I felt anger, sadness, and fear all at the same time. I was deeply angry that I had had to go through so much pain before finally meeting my teacher; that apartheid had made it almost impossible for me to meet with a traditional sangoma woman like MaMngwevu; and that her beautiful world of plants, spirits, and natural magic was disrespected by the Eurocentric world. I was afraid of the steps I would need to take from there, but in that moment I also felt great peace.

MaMngwevu said my gift was very strong and I would become a great sangoma medicine man. She said that the gift ran in my family, which was the only way for someone to have the calling with such veracity. And this was true. My grandmother from Ireland, Mammy Kelly, had a prophetic gift—and predicted the fall of apartheid.

MaMngwevu gave me specific evidence about my life and showed me how the spirit world was calling me. It was as though the wind, soil, medicinal herbs, and animals in her divination room were using her as their voice. In that moment, all of life was witnessing me and calling me to follow my destiny. I had no choice but to listen.

MaMngwevu looked directly at me again and said in isiXhosa, *"Uyafuna ukuba ligqirha? Ndingakuqeqesha."* (Do you want to become a sangoma? I can train you.)

"What does it mean to become a sangoma?" I asked.

*"Xa uligqirha awusayi kuphinda ugule. Uya kuba namandla kwaye uya kunceda nabanye abantu."* (To be a sangoma means you will stop being so sick. You will become strong, and also you will be able to heal people in different ways.)

I replied with a resounding "Yes!" I then asked her to please talk to her ancestors and tell them to go easy on me, that I had my final exams in a few months' time. I explained that my university degree had been interrupted by a strong spiritual emergence a few years earlier, that I had "lost the words" and had to drop out of university for two years. "I accept the calling," I finished, "but I can only give it my full attention once I finish my final exams."

With great compassion, MaMngwevu said again, "*Ahh, Thixo, Nkosi yam, uxolo. Ndiza kuba xelela ukuba umsebenzi wakho uza kuqala xa kuphela unyaka.*" (Oh Lord, my God, I am sorry. I will tell them we will begin your apprenticeship at the end of the year.)

I later learned that she had not finished her schooling because of her own sangoma calling, and that this is a common experience among sangomas and other spiritual/psychic people the world over.

Then MaMngwevu said, "*Ubuye ngomso uze kufumana iintsimbi ezimhlophe. Ungathanda isikhumba sesiphi isilwanyana?*" (Come tomorrow for your first white beads. What animal skin would you like on the end?) I was struck by that; I wasn't sure what she meant. So I asked Thandisizwe to get MaMngwevu to explain.

"*Uphethwe yintwaso iminyaka esixhenxe, umamela amaphupha akho, ngoku uza kuba ngumkhwetha wam. Maxa wambi sisebenzisa isikhumba sebhokhwe kule ndawo ziphela kuyo iintsimbi. Isikhumba sesilwanyana simele isilwanyana esisikhokelayo. Wena ubona eziphi izilwanyana kumaphupha akho?*" As you have been surviving on your own with the thwasa illness for more than seven years and listening to your dreams, you will be one of my senior students," she said in isiXhosa. "Sometimes we put goatskin on the ends of our beads. The skin represents our animal spirit guides. What animals do you see in your dreams?"

I said I didn't have a feeling for goats at that point but had experienced many dreams about baboons.

MaMngwevu nodded her head in understanding. "*Ndiza kufaka isikhumba semfene ezintsimbini zakho kwaye uza kusikelelwa, ukhokelwe ngabantu behlathi.*" (I will put some baboon skin on the end of your white beads, then, so you will be blessed and guided by the spirit of the bush and forest people.)

MaMngwevu mentioned the word *umbilini* to describe the shaky feeling in my body, saying it was part of the thwasa and was a call from the ancestral spirit world and from the Great Spirit, uThixo. I felt the truth in her words as a sensation I sometimes felt if I had drunk too much coffee, and my hands shook. I also experienced this nervous tension as waves of energy moving up and down my body accompanied by occasional feelings of elation, joy, or infinite sadness. Often the umbilini experience made it difficult for me to sleep, and I drifted in the sea of dreams, experiencing lucid dreaming and psychic phenomenon. And I could sense other people's pain and joy, as well as that of animals.

The ancient yogis in India speak of the kundalini as the movement of energy from the base of the spine upward toward the crown of the head. They liken it to a snake coiled at the base of the lower back that awakens and starts to move up the spine when there is a spiritual emergence. As it moves, the individual experiences a range of physical sensations—emotional, psychological, and psychic. I had studied the old writings on kundalini as a way to explain my own spiritual emergence, so it was interesting to note the similarity between the words umbilini and kundalini. This did not seem unusual because MaMngwevu's people, the Xhosa, are one of the oldest indigenous cultures in the world today.

As we left MaMngwevu's home and drove back to town, I felt powerful, strong, excited as never before—and afraid. I was crossing over from my familiar Western world to the traditional African world of healing, dreams, and magic. I felt adrenaline surging in my body, readying me for this leap of faith. Yet questions and concerns flooded my mind.

For starters, I didn't speak isiXhosa—I couldn't even converse with my new teacher. It is an incredibly difficult language to master, and I knew I would have to become proficient in it in order to develop a relationship with MaMngwevu and the Xhosa community. And what would my friends and family think of my decision to devote years to completing this training in another culture? The shift I would have to make was enormous.

There were no white people in the township I had just visited, and the community, which consisted of my university and other institutions, was not sympathetic, tolerant, or open to African traditional customs. Apartheid was only about four years behind us, and the atmosphere was still tainted with distrust between the races.

Most people, however, were tired of all of this, and love and hope were in the air, sparked and ignited by Mandela. People were just beginning to get used to living together without police and army restrictions and to understand that we were all equal under the laws of the land. Still, valuing another person's culture as you valued your own in the new South Africa was a long way off.

It was within this socio-cultural stew that I tentatively began to immerse myself in the culture of Xhosa medicine.

I asked Thandisizwe to keep our experience with MaMngwevu confidential. I knew my university professors and fellow students would be interested only from a purely academic point of view, and I was a private person; I was not prepared to endure their questioning. I had to first integrate the sacred, holy words of Mama and hold them close. I knew that when I was ready to talk to my white friends and family—to "come out" in Western culture—I would.

The morning after my life-changing meeting with MaMngwevu, I found a neatly folded white goatskin outside the meditation room of our Zen center. The skin was fresh and felt slightly damp. Though there were many dogs around, none of them had touched it.

I immediately ran to fetch Thandisizwe, who worked at the university, and then we rushed to Mama's home, showed the skin to her, and told her I had found it outside the room where I prayed. She felt it, said that she had not sent it, and became very quiet. Her face took on the appearance of stone and her voice came from the depths of the earth, "*Izinyanya zivumile, uza kuthwasa ngendlela yasendulo. Mandulo kwakubanje kubakhwetha.*" (The ancestors have accepted you. You will be trained in the old ways. This is what used to happen to apprentices many years ago.)

I was silenced for a moment by the gravity of what I was undertaking. I knew what I wanted—or rather, what I did not want. I did not want MaMngwevu to make things easier for me in any way because I was from another culture. I said to her with passion, "I agree to be your student and train to be a sangoma on one condition—that you train me as if I were a Xhosa man!"

"Of course," she said. "*Ayikho enye indlela.*" (That is the only way.)

MaMngwevu then presented me with my first white beads with baboon skin on the end. She delicately placed the beads around my neck, clasping the front near my throat. I felt like a prince in a royal lineage, a lineage of natural medicine, spirits, and dreams. A shiver went down my spine as my inner wilderness of ancient Africa was born.

I was prepared to go through whatever I needed to in order to fulfill my vocation with dignity. I was prepared to follow not just my teacher, but my fellow Xhosa sangoma apprentices in this ancient way. As they prepared medicinal plants, so would I. As they slept on the floor, so would I. Years later my strong conviction reaped rewards greater than gold as I continued to learn about ubunzulu bobuntu, the sacredness of what it means to be human, according to the Xhosa nation.

In my third interview with MaMngwevu, I met Noluthando (the one with love), her senior student, who welcomed me with a warm smile. She had a noble, dignified demeanor, like a princess in a royal family. Her face was painted with white clay, in keeping with Xhosa sangoma trainees, and her clothes were spotless. She wore a blue dress with finely embroidered Xhosa patterns depicting a traditional person carrying water on her head. She had white beads around her neck, wrists, and ankles. She was pounding medicinal herbs into a fine pulp. I was amazed by her strength as she brought a heavy, round rock down onto a mixture of roots on a flat stone. The clicks of MaMngwevu's isiXhosa speech and the *clink, clink* of the stones mixed together in a wonderful rhythm.

I breathed in the smells of raw herbs as they opened themselves to heal. I felt like part of the aromatic medicine mixture inside the mortar and pestle. Noluthando pounded the herbs, MaMngwevu spoke, and the little children from the street played inside and out. I was hot and shaky, as though I was being cooked in the heady herbal mixture, and I was anxious and excited to know what I would turn into.

After this session with MaMngwevu, I experienced varying emotions, from being tired and drained to elated and almost euphoric—a pattern I would experience for many years. She spoke directly to my spirit, cutting through my doubts and questioning mind.

Thandisizwe and I were led inside the house, where MaMngwevu's family members offered us tea. A tray carrying milk, sugar, and mugs of tea was presented to us with dignity and respect. It didn't matter that the mugs were chipped and the poverty of the people was evident. I was welcomed with grace and a conscious awareness that I had not experienced before in South Africa. These people were awake in the fullest possible sense.

MaMngwevu introduced me to her husband, Tat' uSukwini, a short man with Khoisan features and a very expressive face. He emanated compassion, warmth, and humility, and when he spoke everyone looked up and listened attentively. He brought light and laughter into the faces of the people in the room. Like MaMngwevu, he came from a long line of traditional healers and sangomas, and he was an *induna*,

John with his elders, Tat' uSukwini, MaMngwevu,
Tata uMngwevu (brother), and Tat' Bongani (standing).

or head man, in the Sukwini clan. As such, he was often called upon to officiate traditional ceremonies and was one of the elder men involved with initiating the Xhosa boys into men.

Like Zen masters of old, Tat' uSukwini had a humble job; he was a manual laborer in a nearby town, cutting grass between the main roads. Although he and his family were poor, he never turned anyone away. Visitors always received tea and food if there was any. Elder men and women from various Xhosa families and clans often gathered in his home to talk to him about family matters. He always listened and helped if he could.

Tata looked directly into my eyes and then at the goatskin on my lap while Thandisizwe told him the story of how I came to possess it. He smiled warmly at me and said, "*Wamkelekile apha. Likhaya lakho elitsha eli. Khululeka nanini na ufuna ukuza apha.*" (You are always welcome here. This is your new family. Whenever you want to come here, the door will always be open to you.) I felt like bursting into tears.

He accepted me completely and gave me enormous strength.

I had never experienced such warmth and kindness from people outside my immediate family. I knew from all my travels that people say many things without really meaning them. But I felt the truth of Tat' uSukwini's words, and as the years went by he never faltered from that initial first invitation.

I once had a conversation with the great Credo Mutwa, Zulu sage and high sangoma. When I showed him a picture of Tat' uSukwini and MaMngwevu, he said, "This man has the face of the old Xhosa kings, and his wife has so much suffering in her face. She is a great sangoma."

My Xhosa teachers became my adoptive parents, and they displayed nobility in the truest possible way. They lived by their word and now I would live by it too.

Three weeks into my apprenticeship, MaMngwevu had a powerful dream: her ancestors had come to her and told her what name to give me. They said I was to be called Cingolweendaba, meaning "a messenger or bridge between people and/or cultures." *Cingo* means "wire" in English and *iindaba*, "spiritual news." My name was likened to the image of a telephone line connecting people over long distances. MaMngwevu was very excited and said it was a powerful, auspicious name. It meant I was to be a bridge between the spirit world and people, like a prophet, as well as between people in this world. It spoke about my future work in both: helping communicate spiritual knowledge from the ancestral world through dreams and visions and bridging the divide between Western and black culture in South Africa. At that time I had no idea that I would eventually also travel the Western world teaching South African mysticism.

A few weeks after I met MaMngwevu, she organized a simple naming ceremony for me at her house. A small group of people gathered, including sangomas and local community members. As Mama gave me my new beads, the community responded with a chorus of singing, dancing, and ululating. There was a magical feeling in the air. I knew I was touching something deep inside of me—my destiny was being realized. Although I missed South Korea and my time with my Buddhist teachers, I believed that I was in the right place and doing my work for this lifetime. I was overwhelmed with gratitude and joy. I also felt happy in my heart that I had listened to my dreams and all the signs in my life that had pointed me in the direction of MaMngwevu and her humble home and community.

As the hours moved toward evening, the street sounds softened. Then a loud knock shook us out of our conversations. Two women appeared at the door wearing yellow beads around their necks. They were sangomas from a mystical sect and said their ancestors had encouraged them to knock on this door, telling them something unusual was happening here. The women were greeted with great reverence. MaMngwevu explained that they had entered a small naming ceremony to welcome a new sangoma into the community. The ladies looked at me, smiled beatifically, and blessed me. They agreed with MaMngwevu and our small family that my name was auspicious and that the ancestors had a big plan for me. The room was alive with spirits and quiet dreams.

My journey to marry my inner landscape with the world had begun.

# 6

# Xhosa Culture

## Historical Background

To understand someone's story, you need to understand where they come from and what struggles and challenges they have had to overcome. For the past two hundred years, my adopted Xhosa family had experienced a particularly difficult time, mostly due to white colonialism. This made my presence in traditional Xhosa sangoma ceremonies hard to stomach for many Xhosa people, until they got to know me personally. But as the name Cingolweendaba that MaMngwevu dreamed for me reflects, I am a bridge between cultures, so in this chapter I want to share a brief chronicle of the ancient Xhosa lineage and its modern history.

According to the national 2011 census, isiXhosa-speaking people make up about 16 percent of all South Africans, approximately eight million people. Traditional Xhosa territory runs from Cape Town up the east coast toward the Transkei coast.

The Xhosa are part of the larger Nguni tribe, which in turn is part of the larger group of Bantu peoples who originally moved southward from central and east Africa about three hundred to four hundred years ago. As the Nguni migrated south, they met the Khoisan people, and their mixing resulted in the Xhosa nation that we know today.

The Khoisan, loosely termed "Bushmen," were the original inhabitants of Southern Africa and comprised two groups of people, the Khoi and San. They shared similar physical and linguistic characteristics, setting them apart from the larger Bantu tribes. The Khoi, previously known as Hottentots, were pastoralists and kept cattle. The San were hunter-gatherers. Most of the rock art paintings around Southern Africa were done by San Bushmen during trance states. The Khoisan lived mostly along the coastal regions and are said to be one of the oldest indigenous cultures in the world today.[1]

Southern Africa plays an important part in world history because it is reputed to be the birthplace or origin of modern humans. Evidence for these claims is found in genetic diversity and an incredible array of archaeological artifacts. Some have been found in caves near the sea. Examples of these finds are seen near Mossel Bay, a small coastal town about five hours east of Cape Town. People living in these caves are thought to have been Khoisan people who are believed to have survived the Ice Age by feeding on seafood. Academics maintain that modern humanity originated in these small groups of Khoisan, who then travelled north and populated the world.[2]

It is thought we all have common ancestors in Africa, so it makes sense for us to understand how they saw the world and how they interacted with nature. To them, nature was a living matrix of energy involving the spirits of plants, animals, and people. It was a dreamlike space where everything had meaning, from storms to birdsong.

The Khoisan who weren't absorbed into local communities until more recently were driven inland into the desert regions of Southern Africa and forced to continue the hunter-gatherer lifestyle of their San ancestors. Today most of them live in Botswana and parts of Namibia.

This powerful mixing of Khoisan and Xhosa is seen in the language the Xhosa people speak and in their rich spirituality, filled with metaphor and mysticism. The predominant feature of the Khoisan language is a series of clicks, which to the untrained ear can sound like bird sounds. The isiXhosa language is similar, but with fewer clicks. Anthropologists maintain that the Khoisan people mimic nature and that the language they use is onomato-poeic, with words sounding like the object being referred to. The isiXhosa language is rich in onomatopoeia, heightening the visual effect. Examples are *ukurhona*, meaning "to snore," with emphasis placed on the "rh," sound-ing like *ggg* at the back of the throat. *Iqanda*, meaning "egg," is pronounced with a palatal click on the *q*, imitating the sound of a breaking egg.

## COLONIAL WARS

White presence in South Africa began in 1652 with the Dutch East India Company trading station in Cape Town, which supplied ships with fresh produce. Over time, white people moved inland and claimed ownership of land that was already inhabited by local people, resulting in years of war.

In the late 1700s, English settlers arrived in Cape Town and moved toward the Eastern Cape, which was largely inhabited by the Khoisan and Xhosa people. Battles for land became increasingly bloody and vicious as English forces attempted to secure the land for themselves and drive the local inhabitants farther afield.

A war lasting from 1812 to 1819 culminated in the battle of Grahamstown, when about ten thousand Xhosa warriors surrounded a British fort and attempted to drive the settlers into the sea. The British had rifles and cannons, while the Xhosa had shields and spears—the results were not surprising. Between one thousand and two thousand Xhosa warriors lost their lives, resulting in one of the largest losses of life in Africa at that time.[3] The name for Grahamstown became Egazini (meaning "place of blood" in isiXhosa), in keeping with the Xhosa way of giving names to places to remember important historical events.[4]

History, like life, is complicated. It would be too simplistic to say that the early years in the Eastern Cape were about white people oppressing black people. It would be more accurate to say that it was about all people struggling to feed and house themselves. England had just come through the Napoleonic wars and was rapidly urbanizing. Industrialization was creating a large, extremely poor working class. Shipping people off to colonies like South Africa was a way to deal with insufficient land, too many jobless people, short life expectancy, and poor quality of life. Both the Xhosa and English settlers were caught up in a situation beyond their control and not of their making, both pawns to the imperialistic English upper class.

Sadly, the conflict between white settlers and local black people continued for almost two hundred years. The white minority's dominance of the political and socioeconomic landscape became institutionalized in the form of apartheid. As noted earlier, apartheid is an Afrikaans word meaning "separate development." The name Afrikaans means "African" in Dutch, and the Afrikaans language was originally used by the Dutch settlers and indentured workers brought to South Africa's Cape Province by the Dutch East India Company.

Apartheid's draconian laws only increased the bitterness and misunderstanding between peoples. It did, however, have one interesting positive aspect: while other traditional cultures succumbed to Westernization, African traditional culture in Southern Africa (such as the sangoma culture) not only survived but also thrived. It became a testament to the human spirit rising above adversity. With its focus on Ubuntu, it represents a different form of philosophy and spirituality, with a deeply inclusive psychology, involving man, nature, and the departed. With Ubuntu as a way of life, African spiritual technology—including a diverse range of herbalists, prophets, and faith healers—was a refined and intricate system, vastly superior to Western colonialism's approach of taking and plundering.

Unlike many colonized places around the world, the South African story had a happy ending. In 1994 we had our first democratic elections, and Nelson Mandela, the long overdue answer to white minority rule, became president. As a Xhosa man with Khoisan blood, he represented an end to colonialism and a return to the principles of Ubuntu. His politics radiated forgiveness and reconciliation, and he popularized the term Ubuntu, which in essence is a counterweight to greed and the excesses of capitalist egoic individualism. It speaks about community and the circle of humanity. It says that we are all products of our environment and the communities that raised us.

Nelson Mandela was more than just one man. He was the voice of millions of people, of a timeless culture that survived some of the harshest weather conditions and socio-political chaos the world has ever seen. He became living proof that an indigenous worldview with its focus on community, nature, and the spirit world (in the form of ancestors) can thrive in the modern world. Ubuntu became a model for how to live together in harmony with a focus on togetherness and not limited by selfishness.

# 7

# Xhosa Mysticism

Xhosa mysticism is based on several powerful and cherished principles. I relate them to you here as I encountered them during my apprenticeship, learning to bridge the everyday and the dreamtime, Western culture, and African traditions. My challenge was learning to move like the leopard between worlds.

## THE CONCEPTS OF UBUNTU AND IZINYANYA

As mentioned previously, the essence of Xhosa spirituality and mysticism revolves around Ubuntu. The medicine teachings I learned are called ubunzulu bobuntu, the depth of humanity. The traditional Xhosa sangoma apprenticeship I underwent involved an education of experience and doing, not the Western approach of questions and answers. We learn through mixing the herbs, attending to our teacher and clients, and listening to our dreams. I learned that the heart is the engine and spiritual center of life, and when the drum is played it becomes the uniting voice and heart of the community. Xhosa rhythms and ceremonies mirror the steady pulse and beat of the African landscape, awakening the memory and essence of life.

Ubuntu, like life, is seen as a circle of which we are all a part, including the dead. The ancestors are an important part of the circle because without our memory of them and our connection to our blood lineage, we lose our sense of immortality and then we fear death.

A human being exists through other people, not as an isolated entity. A well-known proverb among the Xhosa people is "*Umntu, ngumtu, ngabantu.*" (A person becomes a person through other people.) The core idea behind Ubuntu is "I am what I am because of who we all are." Each person is responsible for the circle of community, no matter what their status. Ubuntu is an ever-evolving state of being in which people realize their humanity through acts of kindness and compassion and through remembering their ancestors.

I was blessed to receive these ancient teachings via transmission and word of mouth from my sangoma elders in the Eastern Cape. Within them lie the seeds of greater human emancipation and spiritual freedom.

We often use the term *umsebenzi*, "spiritual work," when we refer to sangoma ceremonies to honor our ancestors. When we honor our ancestors, we *khanya*, "shine." The ceremonies are also called *ukukhanya komsebenzi*, "the shining work," because as we connect to our ancestors and the spirit inside us, we start to shine. And this shining helps reconnect us to our spirits, all people, and the world around us.

Interestingly enough, in South Korean Buddhism they say, "The Buddha is not clever—he is shining." All of life is seen to possess Buddha-nature, consciousness, or godliness. And all we have to do to connect with the oneness of life around us is to connect with our own Buddha-nature, or shining inside. I see many similarities between my Buddhist background and my sangoma background with its subtle focus on Ubuntu.

Xhosa culture, over hundreds if not thousands of years, has developed an intricate and beautiful practice of remembering the ancestors through prayer, ceremony involving singing and dancing, and animal sacrifice. The isiXhosa language is rich and expressive, and it has many words to denote blood ancestor, from *amathambo* (bones) and *abantu abadala* (old people) to something more mystical, *izinyanya* (silent hidden ones, or nature spirits). People connect to izinyanya through their blood ancestors, thereby acknowledging their roots in the human family. Like an oak tree, the deeper its roots, the taller and more powerful its branches. For people to access the more refined states of dreaming and spirituality, they need to first connect to their blood ancestors.

Izinyanya is a sacred word. In traditional South African culture over two hundred years ago, it was considered very rude—almost blasphemous—to approach God directly in prayer, so people first called on family members who had passed over into the spirit world, asking them for help when facing calamities such as illness, famine, or war. The word izinyanya speaks about the subtle spiritual forces around us and inside us that maintain our life and our human spirit. Our *isidima* (dignity) is contingent on the strength of our connection to our izinyanya, which can include *umoya wezilo* (animal spirits) as well as nature spirits. The Xhosa sangoma system is deeply mystical and animistic, seeing the spirit of nature in everything.

When I first met MaMngwevu, she told me she would only teach me 20 percent of sangoma knowledge and wisdom; the other 80 percent would come from my own relationship with my izinyanya. Her job was to show me how to pray, listen to my dreams, and interpret the signs from my spirits.

Anyone inquiring into African mysticism will hear about ancestors. This serves as a clue to those with a sincere quest in their hearts and minds to discover their destiny and their reason for being. The greatest pilgrimage of all is the journey toward understanding our soul. The stronger the question "Who am I?" the deeper the quest. Often our soul speaks to us through pain and suffering. Our hidden gifts and life's calling are mysteriously linked to what touches us deeply. The sharper the pain, the greater the opportunity to live and shine.

Our flesh rests on our bones. To connect with our soul, we need to connect deeply with our bones. As a tree connects with its roots and reaches deep into the earth, so human beings have a responsibility to connect with their bones, and our bones are a living embodiment of our ancestry and ancestors. Hence, in the isiXhosa and isiZulu languages the word for bones (amathambo) is also used in reference to ancestors. It is often said that if people want to understand their life path, it is a good idea for them to remember their childhood and their natural tendencies and gifts. Understanding where we come from and developing a relationship with our ancestors is the next level to greater spiritual emancipation.

Our ancestors gave us the gift of life. Through honoring them, we pay homage to the wisdom of our race going back to time before time. In our modern times we face a crisis of forgetting. As we forget our ancestors and where we come from, we also forget our gifts and the incredible beauty and grace that being human offers us. For we are all born to dream and make magic with our hands, voices, and feet. We are the creators of this world, and to tap into our remarkable birthright we need to remember what it means to be human. This journey is an intricate process that begins with the simple action of listening to our own heart and allowing that energy to spread into the world.

Cultures around the world have practiced ancestral veneration since prehistory (over five thousand years ago). Ancestral veneration is connected to our natural inclination to procreate. The silent whisperings in our blood speak about the voices that make us, our mothers and fathers. Ancestors are remembered in the same way a new mother dreams of her future children.

European missionaries and colonizers misunderstood early African spirituality because they were so focused on converting the people to Christianity. Traditional healers and spiritualists were seen in a negative light because they supposedly "didn't know God" or didn't encourage prayers to God. But in traditional Southern African spirituality, people revered and respected God to such an extent that they felt it prudent to use their ancestors as intermediaries. As Christianity took root in Africa, these ways changed to adapt to the status quo. Nowadays people feel comfortable connecting with the Great Spirit, uThixo, directly, but they still include their ancestors in their prayers to show gratitude for the sanctity of life. During sangoma rituals, I have always noted a sense of grace and humility overcome people who pray to their ancestors with an open heart. As we remember our fathers and mothers, we seem to remember our own place in the circle of life, resulting in a profound sense of belonging and openness.

## A SACRED PORTAL—
## THE KRAAL, OR UBUHLANTI

As is true of ancient India, the essence of Xhosa spirituality revolves around the sacred cow. Cows or oxen are seen as a source of wealth, both material and spiritual. In traditional homes, the family cattle are held in a structure known as a *kraal*, or *ubuhlanti* (literally translated as "human forest"). The kraal is a circular structure made from thorns or tree saplings. Traditionally the thorns were used to protect the cattle and other animals from predators such as lions and leopards.

In the center of the kraal is a forked totem pole, known as an *ixhanti*, that reaches up to the heavens, acting as a spiritual conductor. To the right of the entrance to the kraal are a number of animal horns, each representing an animal that has been sacrificed to the ancestors. This represents the spiritual doorway to the ancestral or spirit world; as people pass by the horns they say a prayer to honor their ancestors. And so the kraal is a sacred structure, or portal, used to connect to the ancestors and uThixo.

The Ngwevu family kraal.

We connect with our humanity by standing in a circle in the kraal and honoring our blood ancestors. We all face the ixhanti. We bless its base with brandy and tobacco, activating it with energy. We direct all our prayers to it and it reflects the prayers in all directions. We honor and praise our blood ancestors, the Great Spirit, and our teachers or spiritual lineages. Spiritual lineage is important because the wisdom that is passed down through the generations gives us a means to find our way back home, to the source of life, the dreamtime.

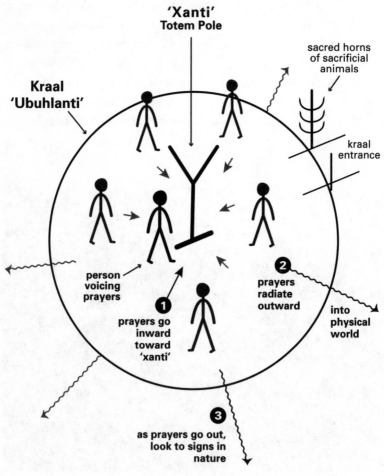

Depiction of people praying in the kraal.

Our prayers are like waves; we direct them inward and then wait for a response from nature. We observe nature as we pray to ascertain the response from the ancestral realm—which is often immediate. Certain birds come into the kraal to denote that the ancestors have heard us; the wagtail, for instance, is a common ancestral bird. Or we look at the movement of nearby animals, such as cows, stray dogs, and goats. If birds or animals move in a particular way, it means that the ancestors have heard us. I have often seen birds fly down next to us and sing, as if the ancient ones are talking in the language of spirits.

Prayer from the heart using the voice is a physical act of love. The words never die; they gather and move into the next world. After we have prayed and observed nature, we sleep and track our prayers in the dreamtime. We may dream of our izinyanya in the form of animal spirits—this is a sign that our prayers have been heard. Often roads are opened or new ones forged from our dreams into our physical world. Our dreams are a sacred pond reflecting our lives and take us into new spaces where we rediscover our humanity.

Honoring our bones and our ancestors is about honoring the sacredness of life. When we do this from a heartfelt, dignified place, we are blessed with dreams that direct us on our life path. We all come from the dreamtime, or cosmic plasma of universal consciousness—heady words that point to an empty space of nothingness, like the stillness in a pond. Approaching this stillness with openness, surrender, and humility helps us connect with our own soul—the part of us that is always alive, constantly connected to the source of life, the dreamtime. When we dream, we plug into the source of life. When we pray in an active, natural way as I've described, we activate our inner dreamer, our soul. Life and death merge, becoming a circle; hence, the kraal space, or ubuhlanti, is realized. As we pray in this way, we connect with more than just our human family. We connect with the plant and animal worlds, the primordial soup of life, and ultimately with the dreamtime, or universal consciousness too.

The isiXhosa words I have introduced you to here describe the heart of Xhosa mysticism: Ubuntu (humanity), ubunzulu bobuntu (depth of humanity), umsebenzi (spiritual work), izinyanya (silent hidden ones), isidima (dignity), umoya wezilo (animal spirits), and amathambo (bones). In the chapters that follow, as I describe my apprenticeship and final initiation, you will meet these essential principles again.

# PART IV

## The Sangoma's Apprentice

# 8

# Xhentsa

## Dancing with the Spirits

## THE THREE PILLARS OF SANGOMA MEDICINE

Sangoma medicine revolves around three interweaving indigenous medicines that aim to activate our spirits and deepen our dreams: *xhentsa*, the trance dance, to stoke the fire of our spirit; *amayeza*, medicinal plants, to cleanse and protect us; and *vumisa*, the art of divination, where we receive guidance, or iindaba, from the spirit world.

I experienced my training as activating my electrical body or spinal cord. Each aspect of the training occurred in a spiral, one step building on another, with prayers weaving everything together like a finely tuned spiritual cord. My journey began with the dance.

The greatest dance is learning to move between the worlds of shadow and light, dreams and reality. The sangoma exists in the twilight world, sometimes seen and sometimes hidden. I had to learn to become like a leopard, to blend into my surroundings and at the same time develop my primal instincts, long hidden from hundreds of years of Westernization. The xhentsa awakened my senses and fueled my inner fire.

Rhythm and music are integral to Southern African spirituality. In the 1800s, a Zulu warrior had to learn how to dance before being tested on the battlefield. The trance dance was used to unite the people and empower their spirits. The drumming rhythms prepared people for war or for healing. The difference was in the *iingoma* (songs or chants) used.

My first recollection of the power of African music and dance is of a time during the South African civil war in the 1980s when I was a teenager. I turned on the six o'clock news and was shocked by what I saw: women and children singing and dancing in front of soldiers in tanks, demonstrating against the injustice of apartheid. They seemed so fearless, armed with their songs, rhythms, and indestructible human spirit. Seeing this, I felt ashamed to be a white person while at the same time impressed with the tenacity of my fellow countrymen. I loved their songs and rhythms and prayed that I could join them one day.

One young man especially stands out in my mind. He was around my age, fourteen or fifteen. He stood at the front of the group of demonstrators confronting the tanks, raising his fist in the air and shouting, *"Amandla!"* (Power!) Each time he did this, the people behind him jumped up and brought their feet down in unison, shouting *"Ngawethu!"* (To us!) The sound of their feet was like a cannon blast to my soul. In my heart I knew two things: one day these people would be free, and I would learn their beautiful rhythms.

In my second interview with MaMngwevu, she told me I would become a great trance dancer. Since she had been correct about so many things in my life over the previous seven years, I was intrigued. I felt on the precipice of a deep transformation that would change not only me but also my whole community. I recall a tangible feeling of electricity in my body.

MaMngwevu invited me to attend a traditional sangoma ceremony as her new apprentice. She asked me to bring a bottle of brandy. We would bless the ancestors with it, and they would come alive with Spirit and bless the participants by appearing in their dreams.

I was nervous as the only white trainee at the ceremony, but my fears were quickly eased when Mama's other trainees greeted me. I waited outside until the appropriate time to enter the ceremony, watching stray dogs running after goats and little children running after the dogs;

the joyous engagement of life was hard to ignore. Everything was moving to the rhythm of the drums inside. Suddenly the door swung open and someone cried out, "*Bayeza, ngenani ngoku!*" (Come, enter now!)

I was quickly hustled into a crowded room. The furniture had been removed, and there were low benches against all the walls. The elder men sat on the left side, the initiated men in the middle, and the elder women on the right. The remaining women sat on straw mats on the ground in front of the elders.

The drums were amazing! The very earth, walls, and air pulsed to their heartbeat rhythm. And the singing was pure heaven. There were mostly women and children in the room, and large ladies dancing and singing in the center of it. They were *jubilant* in every sense of the word. I could sense their spiritual power and strength in their full acceptance of themselves. They had huge breasts and buttocks, attributes that only accentuated their rhythm. Suddenly two of them grabbed me, one grasping each hand. They muttered something in isiXhosa, translated as "You have white beads. You are a sangoma and are not allowed to sit down. You must dance!" I felt very shy in the packed room with all eyes on me, but their jovial, friendly nature put me at ease.

The two ladies danced as their voices soared toward the heavens. When they stomped their feet, I felt the earth shake. One lady took me by my left arm, and another took me by my right. Body contact was no problem, and as their breasts heaved up and down like ships on the sea, I got it! I got the rhythm—I could feel it as they held me fast. As I followed my new teachers, the rhythm held me like a raft at sea. I breathed in and sang the words—and my spirit flew!

My new community was amazed to see me dance. And in my heart of hearts I knew MaMngwevu's words were true. One day I would soar with the eagles as the drums rolled.


## NEW BEADS

I received new white beads, which I wore as two strands around my wrists and ankles. White represents the color of uThixo and the ancestors, and this was a sign that I had accepted my calling and was in service to my ancestors and the spirits moving through my dreams. When I went to sleep at night, I wore my beads and they helped balance and protect my spirit while I entered the other worlds.

As I drove up the hill each day and passed people walking to town, I saw scores of sangomas wearing white beads. I started to understand the subtle language involved and was elated to be part of this hidden culture.

The simple action of putting on the beads blessed me and propelled me deeper into the sangoma world of dreams and magic. It also propelled me headfirst into the center of two groups of people who had been at war for more than two hundred years: the Xhosa nation and white colonialists. For a traditional Xhosa person, becoming a sangoma was natural and ordinary. But as a young white man, I felt so alone. There was no one I could talk to except MaMngwevu, who made my experiences sound natural and ordinary.

My visions often occurred in the twilight upon waking and going to sleep. It felt as if I was crossing a hidden threshold and the beads were a passport to this other realm. My room was open to the African savannah. The mysteries of plants and animals entered my room, and all manner of creatures entertained and taught me at night. I could smell the savannah's sweet aroma as I slept. Elephants often appeared in my visions before I drifted off to sleep. One evening I saw a young elephant cowering against my wall. I felt afraid—I hadn't been brought up with all this knowledge. But MaMngwevu told me I was the young elephant, and I was learning how to connect with the African bushveld.

I was starting to wake up and feel.

## A MESSENGER BETWEEN CULTURES: THE BEGINNING OF THE JOURNEY

I was starting to see life through the eyes of a Xhosa sangoma. It was not pretty or easy to stomach. I felt the injustice of being seen as a second-class citizen who didn't adhere to the Western view of life and society. At university and with friends alike, eyes rolled when I entered a room wearing my beads.

My Xhosa sangoma friends felt disempowered. Yes, South Africa was democratic by now and led by Nelson Mandela, but African mysticism was still misunderstood and marginalized. Thus, my beads brought other lessons and unwanted attention. I did not discuss such issues with MaMngwevu—there was no need to. They were all around us, an aura of fear and distrust we had to work hard to diminish.

Most of the time when Xhosa people in town saw me and my sangoma beads, I saw a tapestry of emotions flood their faces. A Xhosa cashier at the local supermarket, for example, noticed my beads and asked me why I was wearing them. I said in isiXhosa, "*Mna igqirha.*" (I am a sangoma.)

"But it is not possible for white people to become sangomas," she replied.

Then it was my turn to get emotional. "Do you know Archbishop Desmond Tutu?"

"*Ewe, ndiyamazi.*" (Yes, of course.) Everyone knew the well-respected archbishop, a champion of democracy in South Africa and part of the Xhosa nation.

"Well, he is an English priest. Do you think it is okay for a Xhosa man to become an English priest?"

"Of course!"

"Then it must be okay for white people to become Xhosa priests. I am a Xhosa priest, a sangoma."

Often we conversed in the isiXhosa language. Some cashiers smiled and said they had learned something new, while others clicked their tongues and angrily said, "It is not possible for white people to become sangomas. They have no ancestors!" At times like this, feeling frustrated and dispirited, I simply gathered my milk and bread and walked away.

In the first few years of my apprenticeship, this was the norm. White people frowned at me and Xhosa people felt I was stealing from their culture. My dreams and calling were private and I didn't feel I had to continually justify myself to strangers, so I chose to wear only a few beads into town. I became like the leopard, seen only by those who needed to see me—my immediate family, Xhosa family, sangoma colleagues and community, and clients who needed healing.

I developed a close friendship with Thandisizwe, who helped interpret my conversations with MaMngwevu. She spoke in an older, more traditional isiXhosa that is found in the farm areas around the Eastern Cape. I had learned isiXhosa at university, but I was far from proficient. And when Mama got excited and her energy was up, she spoke very fast, with a whirl of clicks. At times such as this I looked at Thandisizwe for clarification.

Thandisizwe was a charming man who everyone loved. He was an incredible listener, and his English was excellent. MaMngwevu's life wasn't easy, and sometimes when she was in a heavy mood you could feel thunder in the air. She was responsible for educating and looking after at least two grandchildren as well as children from other relatives who were struggling with poverty and left their children with Mama for safekeeping. On days when she was fraught with worry, her face brightened at the sight of Thandisizwe. With his perpetual sunny disposition, he could always make her laugh.

Thandisizwe could translate from isiXhosa to English like no one I had seen before—effortlessly. Still, the language was very idiomatic, often referring to cultural symbols or metaphors. We spent hours discussing MaMngwevu's interviews so I could understand what she was referring to.

Thandisizwe told me he had never been as close to a white man as he was with me. I once asked him why he was so willing to help me. He said he had never heard of a white man becoming a sangoma and felt that we were making history together. He was very sensitive to the divisions in South African society and made it known to me that if I ever needed help, his home was open to me. He was true to his word, and we spent hours chatting in his home, about a five-minute drive from MaMngwevu's and in a slightly wealthier part of the township. Thandisizwe loved his Xhosa culture and described the traditional ways to me.

He was amazed by how powerful my dreams were and told me he had never heard of a Xhosa sangoma having such dreams. My interpretations of the dreams and further discussions with Mama and other elders filled him with deep respect for me and my gift. Thandisizwe was in his late thirties, and it was unusual in Xhosa society for a younger man to be invited into council meetings with elders like MaMngwevu and her husband, Tat' uSukwini. So, in a surprising twist, Thandisizwe was learning about his own culture through his experience with me.

In the early days of my sangoma training, the challenge of bridging the two cultures sometimes felt insurmountable and I often questioned my calling. I was caught between two groups of people who were ignorant of one another, an ignorance that often spilled over into anger and hatred. Whenever I was disconsolate with depression, anxiety, and doubt about my calling, Thandisizwe reminded me of my dreams and all the discussions we had with the elders. He thanked me for my courage, love, and respect and told me I was one in a million. He said my gift was larger than me and I had to continue, and that I wouldn't be alone—he would be with me. Thandisizwe gave me hope.

Some days Thandisizwe was like a referee between me and MaMngwevu. I would ask her a question to do with dreams and the sangoma culture and she would keep quiet. But I was stubborn and kept asking her. I felt my spirits moving inside me, and I desperately wanted answers. I had not yet learned that this was not the way things work in a traditional sangoma apprenticeship: the student watches, helps, and listens. Mama and I would stare at each other until she finally agreed to explain things. When the atmosphere got a bit heated, Thandisizwe smiled and broke the ice.

There was huge love between me and MaMngwevu—we just had to learn each other's culture and way of doing things. But the onus was on me; she was my teacher and it was up to me to walk in her culture. I was sick with the thwasa illness and she held the cure.

Over time I asked Mama fewer questions, and the more I helped around the house and worked alongside the other apprentices, the more I found myself assimilating into my new environment.

The engine behind the sangoma way is turned, finessed, and harnessed through the drum and rhythms. In isiZulu, the word sangoma means "person or people (pl.) of the song" because we use rhythms and songs to go into trance. We work with an *isigubu*, a double-sided dancing drum with a strong bass sound that calls the ancestral spirits to us. For me, the sound is pure heaven—it awakens every cell in my body.

The isiXhosa word for a sangoma is different from the isiZulu. I am called an *igqirha*, "the one who holds the lightning rod of the ancestors." The lightning rod is our spines, and we heat the energy of our spines through dancing in a particular way. We dance and go into trance and then give spirit news to the community.

We literally become conductors of lightning energy through our dancing. This is why in certain parts of the Eastern Cape and Transkei, traditional sangoma ceremonies are not performed during a storm; lightning has been known to strike ceremonial homes. The energy the sangomas generate affects nature. I have often seen a calm, cloudless sky at the start of a ceremony give way to wind and rain. We are also known as diviners: water bearers, or rainmakers. In precolonial times, sangomas were called on to welcome the rain during times of drought.

I wore all my beads for our traditional ceremonies. The sangomas and their apprentices were given a place of honor in the home, usually in a room in the back, away from the public. As we sangomas entered the sacred room, we knelt down and greeted the most senior in the group to the most junior, shaking each person's hands by clasping both hands. The senior person would say to me, "*Molo, kunjani?*" (Hello, how are you?) I would respond in isiXhosa, saying, "*Ndiphilile nam, kunjani kuwe?*" (I am fine, how are you?) Then the senior sangoma welcomed me into the home and I was offered food and drink. I felt so much love and acceptance. I wished my fellow white South Africans could witness the grace, love, respect, and etiquette of my dignified sangoma colleagues through my eyes.

Sometimes I witnessed a remarkable thing—a trainee coming close to breaking down as they shook the hands of a senior sangoma because their life was so difficult and their thwasa illness nearly unbearable. In these moments the elder sangoma simply held the trainee's hands and offered quiet words of reassurance and love. The whole room was quiet, and I could sense the movement of Spirit and Ubuntu making us one.

I traveled with MaMngwevu and her apprentices all over the local township and surrounding Eastern Cape, taking part in a number of ceremonies. In the beginning, Thandisizwe joined us and gave me encouragement. He was amazed by the way I moved when I danced. People assumed white people couldn't dance well, so I was often the center of attention—they were curious to see the *umlungu* (white man) dance.

Each ceremony began in the sangoma room, where we gathered our spirits and met one another before joining the community in the main house. As the drums started to roll, I felt a tingle travel down my spine and into my feet. The drumming was always accompanied by iingoma, and the singing was spectacular, with deep harmonies. One sangoma would start, quickly followed by the rest of the group. The most junior trainees would start to dance. Watching them, my body shook with energy. My emotions rose.

In the beginning, I sometimes felt very grumpy. This gave way to a state of anxiety or nervousness. Eventually, I had to get up and dance. My emotions soared and I felt exhilarated, like I was riding an enormous wave out at sea with a feeling of connection to nature and all of life. My heartbeat was so strong that all I felt was my heart and all I heard was the drum, the two sounds seeming to merge together. I felt a profound interconnectedness between all things.

My sorrow and pain from feeling misunderstood as a white South African with a sangoma calling merged with the poverty and pain of my countrymen around me. We sang, all of us together, from the bottom of our hearts. And in the flow of the rhythm, the beat of the drum, and the cry of the collective voices, we became one. I was no longer connected to my personality, my whiteness, blond hair, or blue eyes. I felt permeated with love and peace, as though everything was connected, with meaning beyond all comprehension—from the swishing tails of the dogs outside to the old people sharing a smoke to the young *tsotsis* (gangsters) roaming the streets nearby like sharks.

As my feet moved quicker and quicker, I raised my arms toward the sky, one stick in each hand. Holding the sticks seemed to help whip my body into a higher state, like a bird flapping its wings. I felt like an eagle—soaring, free. My eyes were half open as in Zen meditation, and I kept them focused on a fixed place on the ceiling just above my head. This seemed to steady my breathing and balance my body as I climbed higher and higher with the dance.

I always knew I was in the zone, or the trance state, when I sensed a floating sensation around me and lost the feeling of my body, and for a split second felt only peace and harmony. As I came out of this place, I saw the whites of my community's collective eyes as they witnessed my dancing.

The chants and accompanying rhythms, evocative and hypnotic, had a profound effect on my soul. They transported me to a magical land beyond language, culture, pain, and suffering. In the midst of the chants, I lost myself—I felt transported to the African bush, surrounded by birds, wild animals, and medicinal plants. Waves of energy like small needles traveled up and down my body, and my spirit was renewed and invigorated.

Sometimes the chants were warlike, other times like lullabies sending all of us to the land of dreams. The mere action of clapping my hands and humming to the rhythms elevated my spirit and opened my mind to the dreamtime, the ancestral world beyond life and death.

During traditional sangoma gatherings, known as an umsebenzi, each sangoma is given a chance to dance to their favorite spirit song so they can receive iindaba from the ancestral world. After I had been with my teacher for a few weeks, it was my turn. A young lady, or *sisi* (sister), asked me in isiXhosa what my song was: "*Ithini ingoma yakho?*"

The first words that popped into my head were "*Kwan Se-um Bo-sal,*" from the Buddhist chant I had learned in South Korea devoted to the Buddhist saint, or bodhisattva, Kwan Se-um Bo-sal (known as Guanyin and other names in different parts of Asia). She asked me to sing it.

I sang: "Kwan Se-um Bo-sal, Kwan Se-um Bo-sal, Kwan . . ."

One of the sisis picked up the drum. The whole group soon followed me. Then people outside who heard us singing joined us.

Now the whole room sounded like a South Korean temple with everyone joining in the Kwan Se-um Bo-sal chant.

My beloved Zen master was with me in spirit; in my mind's eye I could see him smiling. With no plan to do so, I was demonstrating the connection he had spoken about: that white and black people needed to connect as human beings, to go beyond the boundary of race that was tearing us to pieces.

After we finished, there was a roar of excitement and I felt the love of my new community. One of the sisis said to me in isiXhosa, "Thank you for teaching us your song. Now we will teach you ours." And from that day on I was taught Xhosa sangoma chants to both open and empower my spirit and my community.

The community always asked the sangoma what their ingoma was so they could sing for them and help the sangoma connect with the spirit world. Then the sangoma went into trance and received visions and messages for the community. Once they had received these messages and it was time to honor and praise their ancestors, the sangoma shouted, "*Pheza!*" (Stop!) and raised their arm. The junior sangomas knelt on the ground and praised their ancestral spirits while the seniors stood. After the praising was completed, the sangoma gave their iindaba, or news, to the community.

Singing my ingoma always left me feeling raw and vulnerable but intimately connected to the world around me. I could feel the poverty and pain of my adopted community. I could also feel their deep connection to their ancestors and the natural world—a regal, golden connection.

During these moments I spoke about the power of the Xhosa traditional culture, that the people still remembered their ancestors, dreams, and medicinal plants. I told the community they were deeply blessed by uThixo because they remembered these things and where they came from. I honored the Xhosa ancestors and people for allowing me to enter the sacred crucible of their culture. In my heightened state of awareness, a voice, image, or wind known as *umoya* (spirit) passed through me. I felt the deep sense of hopelessness that poverty and diseases like AIDS and tuberculosis brought to the townships and informal settlements around the Eastern Cape. The diseases brought death, and the community was in a constant state of bereavement, with funerals happening every weekend.

There is no word in isiZulu or isiXhosa for depression, only *umoya ophantsi*, meaning "spirit energy down." The job of the sangoma is to help lift the spiritual energy of the individual and community, and the mark of good umsebenzi (spiritual work) is *umoya ophezulu* (the community feeling uplifted spiritually). We do this through

Xhentsa: John wearing full beads, dancing at a traditional
Xhosa ceremony to connect with the ancestors in 2012.

dancing, singing, drumming, and giving iindaba, focusing on the truth of what is happening to people and channeling messages from the ancestral world.

The visions I received stressed the importance of encouraging the community to look to their own traditions, ancestors, and dreams for answers to their material poverty rather than relying on the Western world. I saw the richness of the culture and the spiritual strength of the people. A voice emerged from the deepest part of me and, speaking in fluent isiXhosa, I shouted, *"Zingceni ngenkcubeko yenu!"* (Be proud of your culture!) In the heat of the dancing I had visions of the Xhosa ancestors coming toward me with smiles on their faces and speaking to me in isiXhosa, visions that flowed with the dreams I had experienced during preceding nights. These messages were clear: "Tell the people to remember who they are and not to forget us, their ancestors. Tell the people to believe in us and if they are suffering to call on us for help. We are here for them."

Once, a word came to me from the mist of the trance state—*masiy' embo* (let us remember the old ways)—and the Xhosa ancestors from the other world smiled and nodded encouragingly to me.

I cried out, "masiy' embo!"

The community answered me: "masiy' embo!" and followed my iindaba with a well-known ingoma called "masiy' embo." I had not known the word was also a chant. My visions shone as they chanted and the Xhosa ancestors carried on smiling at me. Masiy' embo is an old word that speaks about Ubuntu and the need to remember both our ancestors and the richness of our human birth.

I finished my iindaba with *"Enkosi kakhulu, mawethu."* (Thank you, ladies and gentlemen.) The people's faces shone—I had done my job. The room was in a state of umoya ophezulu, the spirit of the community lifted high. They had heard my message, and my skin color was irrelevant. All they saw when they looked at me was a sangoma.

Rhythm and song are the lifeblood of the sangoma culture and represent one of the most important ways we connect to Spirit. After one particular initiation ceremony, I returned home to Johannesburg to spend time with my parents. I meditated before sleeping and woke in the early hours with a vivid dream. In the dream I saw a drum standing before me with strange black and white markings. A lady's voice spoke to me: "Every sangoma needs a drum. This is yours. Go and get it." I was then given instructions on where to buy this drum in downtown Johannesburg.

I was struck by the power and clarity of the dream. During breakfast I explained my dream to my mother and asked if I could borrow her car to go into town. She immediately said no, fearing crime. But I felt no fear. My dream was clear and I knew which shop to go to. At last my mother relented.

I arrived at the traditional medicine shop I was seeking. It was owned by Mr. and Mrs. Govender, South Africans of Indian descent. At the back of the shop was a small shrine to the elephant god Ganesha, known as the remover of obstacles. I was again reminded of the similarities between Hindu culture and traditional South African spirituality. Sangomas are also known as elephant people because our job is to help remove obstacles for people, to open their roads (*uvula indlela*) so they can realize their destinies in this life and the next.

I asked Mrs. Govender what kinds of drums she had in the store. She brought a few down that didn't match my dream. Then she said, "John, there is only one small drum left up there. I think it could be a bit too small for your uses."

Normally we use large drums for our ceremonies in the township, but my dream drum was smaller than average, just the right size for traveling. When I saw the one she now held, my heart skipped a beat—it looked exactly like the drum in my dream. Mrs. Govender said, "For you, John, I give you special price, and I will include some drumsticks. Try putting tennis balls on the end. They make a wonderful sound." This was a great tip that I appreciated years later.

I was overcome with excitement in the store and started to play a traditional sangoma rhythm on my new drum. As I played, I felt a delightful energy come over me, and I fell into a resonant, hypnotic beat. The sounds reverberated across the shop, waking the spirits in the animal skins hanging from the ceilings. The leopard skins danced and the baboon skulls cried out to me. The selection of herbs in jars turned into a fine mist and enveloped me like a warm blanket. Then the rhythms moved outside onto the streets in a wave of spirits, both animal and plant, flooding the streets with smells and magic. I was transported to a world where the lion is king and the vulture is a messenger of the dead.

I woke to the sounds of people speaking in isiZulu and isiXhosa around me. The shop was filled with people moving around me and dancing. Some entered in a hurry, hearing the sound of the sangoma rhythm, only to click their tongues and exclaim, "*Hayi umlungu!*" (It's a white man!) and quickly leave again. Others remained, pondering this apparition of a sangoma in the skin of a white man. My drum brought healing, magic, and a taste of the ancestral/spirit world. It had a magical, supernatural, timeless quality that helped people reconnect with their spirits. This made sense to me because it had been given to me in my dream. I was overjoyed. And every time I played the drum thereafter, the sound was always fresh, new, and a reminder of the other worlds.

It took more than five years for the local community around MaMngwevu to accept me. The first few years were very difficult. I often felt hatred and anger burning into me like a knife through my soul. But after my years as a Zen student, I felt called to be a bodhisattva, someone who dedicates their life to the removal of suffering. I realized that people didn't hate *me*, John, but only what I represented: white imperialism.

Distrust lingered after the fall of apartheid. In our township, for instance, my teacher was accused of practicing black magic because she had decided to train me. I saw this as a symptom of apartheid, and I believed that every kind action I took would make a difference and that no matter how small it might be, it could help them understand that not all white people were evil.

For her part, MaMngwevu's dream about uThixo the night before meeting me was so strong that it permeated her every action. And no matter how difficult the community pressure was around her, she stood by me and adopted me into her family. The negative voices around us only made us stronger and brought us closer together.

Then one day there was a ceremony in the township during which the hatred toward me was palpable. As I struggled with my emotions and the feelings around me, I looked at MaMngwevu and noticed the same pain in her eyes. The air was heavy, and a darkness rested upon us like a veil.

The drums and singing stopped as Mama raised her hand, indicating her chance to give iindaba to the community. She became like a lioness protecting her young as she pounced around the room, shouting at the top of her voice. I saw fear and wonder in the eyes of the people. My own heart was pounding as electricity shot up and down my spine. MaMngwevu's wide eyes were like burning embers as she shouted from a far place inside her spirit.

She pointed to her wrist, saying, "*Xa unokusika apha, kungaphuma igazi elibomvu.*" (If you cut my arm, red blood flows.)

"*Xa unokusika uCingolweendaba, kungaphuma igazi elibomvu.*" (If you cut John's arm, red blood flows.)

"*Ngamanye amaxesha ndiphupha izinyanya zabelungu, ngamanye amaxesha uCingolweendaba uphupha izinyanya zamaXhosa.*" (Sometimes I dream about the ancestors of white people, and sometimes John dreams about Xhosa ancestors.)

"*Ngaphantsi kwamanzi zonke iintlanga ziyancedana, zisebenzisana kunye. Thina apha emhlabeni sikruthakruthana sodwa. Sonke sinegazi elibomvu kwaye uThixo mnye kuphela.*" (Under the river all the races of man mingle and help each other; however, above the ground we fight one another. We all have red blood and there is only one Great Spirit.)

Then she told the gathering she had visited my parents' home in Johannesburg and that she and her husband were treated very well.

She said that I was very respectful toward her and her family in her home, and I was like one of her children. She shouted these last words with everything she had and stared into everyone's eyes. The message was clear: if the people messed with me, they were messing with one of her own children.

After that, everything was different.

## A PROPHET SPEAKS

One time I took part in a sangoma friend's ceremony. We ended up dancing outside near their kraal, which was filled with cows. My friends, junior sangoma initiates, had their entire faces painted white. There was something ancient blowing in the wind, and when my friends started to dance and stomp their feet into the earth, a dear friend approached me and handed me my new dancing stick covered in beads. I held the stick in both hands and raised it to the heavens like a divining rod and conductor of cosmic energy. Something broke free inside of me as my feet took on a life of their own.

This auspicious moment was punctuated by my sangoma colleagues dancing around me in a circle. Their quick movements energized my own dancing. I danced to a place of stillness within myself. Everything became very quiet. The timeless voice of my own ancestors spoke inside me. It told me to learn all I could from the Xhosa people and to show them the utmost respect. It said one day I would be called to the lands of my blood people in Europe to teach them how to remember their own ancestors. When that time came, I would need to be ready.

As the songs stopped, a man came running toward me with tears in his eyes. He held my hands in his and kissed them passionately. He covered my hands with his tears while looking deeply into my eyes. He spoke quickly in isiXhosa, saying, "*Bendicinga ukuba abelungu abamazi uThixo, kodwa namhlanje ndiyabona ukuba uyamazi uThixo. Ndiyambulela uThixo ngokundifundisa nangokundibonisa wena.*" (For many years I didn't think that white people knew God, but today I see that I was wrong because I see that you know God. Today I am very happy and I am grateful to God for teaching me and showing me you.)

This beautiful man, named Luxolo, was known as a prophet and a dreamer in the community. He was also the local drum maker. There was no way Luxolo could have known the vision I had received, but he certainly felt my spirit stir and touch something beautiful and sacred, and his emotional outpouring was filled with passion and humility. We were all part of that moment and received the healing and guidance we needed. I was struck by the power of the group and by how all our visions were shared and part of the collective human community. I was deeply touched.

At last my work was appreciated, and loved.

# 9

# Amayeza

## Magic Plants

An important part of sangoma apprenticeship is learning how to work with plants. Plants have the ability to cleanse us in body, mind, and spirit. They purify and ground us in the natural world and open us up to the world of spirits—both animal and plant.

My plant world journey started with a few twists of newspaper. MaMngwevu made an intricate performance of throwing handfuls of dried herbs onto a newspaper and then deftly rolling and twisting the paper into a neat block of herbal magic that smelled beautiful. The dried herbs had a life of their own, beckoning and pulling me into their secret world. Mama clicked away in isiXhosa, describing the uses of the plant medicines:

"*Apha uyasela.*" (This is for drinking.)

"*Apha uyavasa.*" (This is for washing.)

"*Apha uyaqhumisa.*" (This is for burning to ward off evil spirits.)

"*Apha uyatshiza.*" (This is for sprinkling your home.)

"*Sithi, 'Hamba moya omdaka!'*" (When we are doing this, we say, "Go away, evil spirit!")

As a spiritual warrior, a sangoma uses the power of prayer and herbs to fight evil and negativity, or *moya omdaka*—"dirty spirit." Moya omdaka can include all forms of negativity: from physical pollution to pollution of the mind by negative emotions, of which jealousy, anger, and hatred reign supreme. We can absorb negative emotions from other people, often unconsciously, and most people are not even aware they are "dumping" negativity on those around them.

Negativity can also be used deliberately, like a weapon, sent toward others in the form of black spells or "black magic"; fortunately, in my experience this is quite rare. In the old colonial days, sangomas were called "witch doctors" because they were thought to doctor the negative effects of the evil spells of witches, who were seen as people who used magic in negative ways. But this didn't reflect the sangomas' deeper, more spiritual job of helping people connect with their vital essence and their dreams, thus realizing their potential in this lifetime. As spirit doctors, sangomas work on the finer, more subtle energies that surround people.

During the amayeza part of my apprenticeship, I learned that washing with plants, drinking plant teas, and sprinkling our living spaces neutralize negativity and bring a sense of peace and groundedness in the here and now. On a physical level, this makes sense. Life as we know it is made up of positive and negative ions. Plants are believed to absorb positive ions, and an excess of positive ions is thought to bring about depression, asthma, and other health-related issues.[1] So it makes sense that one of the oldest herbal systems in the world, sangoma medicine, uses raw, organic plant medicine to bring clarity of body, mind, and spirit.

Plants can have magical and profound effects on our consciousness. I recall once feeling particularly down and heavy after a night of not sleeping, and feeling troubled by spirits during the night. A fellow herbalist prepared a mixture of plants, including a plant bulb that looked like a large onion. She carefully removed the juice and poured a few drops of this "onion juice" onto the crown of my head. I immediately felt an electric shock that traveled all the way down my spine. My lethargy disappeared completely, and the world around me seemed fresh and new, like after a thunderstorm. And later that night my dreams shifted and moved in a different way. I felt a renewed sense of strength and optimism.

The first plant MaMngwevu gave me was *impepho* (the breeze), a form of African sage. It is burned, and its fragrant smoke is passed around to ritually cleanse people before and after sacred ceremonies. To awaken my spirits and have clear dreams, MaMngwevu instructed me to burn impepho before sleeping and pass the smoke around my ears, neck, and the crown of my head. She also encouraged me to breathe in some of the smoke. It has a strong smell and is said to help bring you into and out of trance.

Impepho could be termed a "gateway plant" because it helps open the door to the spirits of the plant kingdom—but it takes an honest and respectful relationship for the door to open. MaMngwevu encouraged me to notice the impepho plant with its little yellow flowers as I walked in the veld, and that when I found the plant to say some prayers and ask for permission from the ancestral world to take some to use in my spiritual practice. I have often found it helpful to also make a small offering of tobacco, which is another gateway plant frequently used by indigenous healers across the globe. Whether we offer tobacco or something else, such as white and blue beads or even our own hair or saliva, the action of giving a gift opens the relationship to the plant kingdom. The earth plane is all about relationships, and friendship is sealed through an attitude of openness, service, and generosity.

My sangoma colleagues and teacher encouraged me to pay attention to my plant dreams. When I was shown particular plants, I was to write down their names, draw them, and focus on their qualities. I learned to feel the spirits of the plants as they came to me.

Strong plant dreams meant spiritual progress. I often went on pilgrimages into the forest to find the plants that I dreamed about. Dreaming the plant and then finding it is a key element of sangoma culture and helps the sangoma bridge the spirit and mundane worlds.

When I found the plants from my dreams, I said prayers to my ancestors and the Great Spirit and made an offering to the plant with either tobacco or small white and blue beads representing a connection to the spirit world. I knelt next to the plant, spoke my name aloud, and honored my ancestral spirits and the spirit of the plant while making my offering. I asked the plant for permission to take parts or all of it to use for my sangoma healing practice. If my prayers and offerings were done in a mindful and humble way, the plant spirits became spiritual allies and could be called upon to help heal people in magical ways.

I included plants I had dreamed about when I made plant mixtures in order to infuse the mixtures with consciousness. This often resulted in potent dreams that might involve my ancestral spirits, plants, and animals.

Incidentally, we sangomas do not generally work with hallucinogenic plant medicine as some other traditions do. Our preference is to let the natural gift of the individual surface without influence from strong intoxicants. However, if people are called in their dreams to work with hallucinogenic plants, they should listen carefully and proceed cautiously, with an experienced plant medicine practitioner to guide them.

The plant world's living consciousness helps wake us up on a cellular level. Passing this consciousness on is akin to transferring electricity, sparking and heating people up. After my clients experienced medicinal plant washes, they often reported feeling warmer and more awake. One client reported to me that he couldn't close his eyes—everything around him was extremely vivid, and all his senses were enlivened.

It is said in sangoma culture that a sangoma should be able to heal people with a handful of grass; it is the sangoma's connection to the spirit world that heals the client. The sangoma's raw, primal, kundalini energy—their heat or lightning energy—is transmitted to the plants through mindful, conscious prayer and then this energy is transmitted to the client. The result could be greater clarity, heat, or a tingling sensation in the body. Sometimes people also experience a stirring in their emotional body. They might report feeling moody, with emotions ranging from euphoria to depression. These are all signs that the plant mixture is working because the client is waking up on a deep, cellular level. I liken the effect of this transfer of lightning energy to the transformation of water into steam. You can think of these rising emotions as steam, a sign that something powerful is happening at the core of our spirits.

John administering medicinal plant foam
to a client's head during a blessing ceremony.
PHOTO COURTESY OF DIANNE TIPPING-WOODS

# 10

# Vumisa

## The Art of Divination

While divination can take many forms, my journey began with vumisa. The word means "agreement." In divination, the context is ancestral agreement. The diviner connects to a person's ancestral spirits and endeavors to feel what is happening to that person. The diviner first describes physical sensations, then emotional and spiritual experiences, and if the diviner senses the person correctly, the person says, "*Ndiyavuma!*" (I agree!)

The wind of life blows through all things. In isiXhosa we speak of umoya—wind, spirit, or soul. In Buddhism everything is seen to have Buddha-nature, or "the shining." All of life has an aspect of the divine within it: the seed of purity or godliness. To divine means to observe with a nonjudgmental eye the condition of a person's soul. A diviner is an empath, someone who feels others' suffering.

I was very nervous the first time I practiced vumisa. It was a hot summer day, and many people were lined up looking for divination. A family of six entered the coolness of the divination room in sacred silence. I was awestruck by their humility and their confidence in my teacher and me. MaMngwevu looked at me with compassion and encouragement. My body was shaking, my palms were sweating, and a strange tingling sensation moved up and down my spine. My job was to identify who in the group was sick and what was wrong with them, and suggest ways to cure them.

I went down on my knees and started praying intensely in isiXhosa, saying my name and praising my ancestors and uThixo. As I did this, I felt a breeze move through me. In my third eye I saw a range of difficult images, feelings, and emotions, and I was filled with sadness and compassion. As I connected with the ancestral spirits of the group, I felt the depth of the people's suffering. My voice changed, becoming deeper and more resonant, and my eyes stared into emptiness. I felt as though a new, wiser, and more powerful spirit was entering me. I bowed down to this spirit with reverence and awe and watched as if from a distance as the divination unfolded.

I recounted nights of nausea and sleeplessness, of nightmares and feeling lost. The people responded with, "Siyavuma!" (We agree). After a while I stared at a young woman at the edge of the group who was having a particularly difficult time. I said she was the one suffering. They all agreed. I felt her pain as if it were my own.

John (center) at one of the initiation ceremonies
during his apprenticeship period.

The wind inside picked up momentum. I closed my eyes, then opened them again, and more words flooded out of me. I described in detail her physical pain and what she was experiencing. Then the wind cooled and was followed by a series of images where the spirits showed me how to help. I saw healing techniques that incorporated drinking and washing with herbs as well as a traditional ceremony to honor the family's ancestors.

I explained to the family that it was important for them to gather and organize a small ceremony to honor their ancestors. The focus should be *ukubulela*, thanking their ancestors for each other and the gift of life. I knew these extremely poor people were focusing on their sense of lack rather than their spiritual strength. Yet their ancestral spirits were very strong and were constantly talking to them. I felt the power of their dreams.

I asked if they dreamed of the old people—their ancestors.

"*Ewe!*" (Yes!) they all replied. But I saw that they had lost faith in their ancestors because they had no money and they felt they had no luck or blessings in their lives. I told them that in giving thanks for their lives, their family, and their dreams, new possibilities would open for them. I saw that their ancestral spirits wanted to help them, but the family was not listening because they were focusing on what they lacked. To this, the family nodded their heads with quiet humility and responded with "*Camagu!*" a term of reverence and respect for a Xhosa sangoma.

I left the family and told my teacher what had happened in my divination. She replied, "*Uthethe inyaniso!*" (You spoke the truth!) We discussed which herbs to give the family to help cleanse them, give them strength, and facilitate a deeper connection with their ancestral spirits. Then she went to talk to the people and answer any questions they might have.

I felt great relief. The shaking sensation in my blood and spine dissipated, and the heat in my palms and forehead eased. The family left with a few bags of herbs neatly wrapped in newspaper, their silence giving way to joyful clicks as they conversed with one another. It had been a powerful experience for all of us—the ancestors had spoken.

I felt their wisdom in the cool sweetness of the divining wind and the transformation in the people around me.

The divining gift develops over time. The repeated practice of prayer, plant medicine, and dancing activated and then enhanced my ability to see clearly. Just listening to my heart, following my breath, giving thanks for the gift of life, and praying to my spirits with love and humility gave me the guidance I needed.

There is a simple but important saying among the Xhosa sangoma people, the *amagqirha*: "*Landela isiphiwo sakho*"—"Follow your gift." Follow your dreams and the messages you receive. The trick, always, is to listen.

I learned that all great gifts carry the burden of responsibility, and every light casts a shadow. Though I hoped to have the strength to embrace my life's calling and the responsibilities it carried, my critical, judgmental mind showed itself in self-deprecating thoughts and feelings of unworthiness, which often left me extremely lonely and depressed. I questioned the wisdom I received in the quiet moments of my day. I worried about my path and my difficulty grasping the isiXhosa language so that I could communicate clearly to the clients coming for divination. I was self-conscious about being different: having white skin and not being a native isiXhosa speaker. My leopard spirit taught me to dance in the shadows of my self-consciousness and to trust in the path my dreams were taking me.

My teacher and her family accepted me as I was, and met my struggle to speak isiXhosa with warmth and patience. And my spirits circumnavigated my chattering mind and gave me dreams that were so powerful that all I could see and feel were the messages they were delivering to me. In the thrall of a dream, self-doubting questions didn't surface, and the dreams left a quiet silence inside, which steadily grew over the years.

One such dream came to me when I had been practicing vumisa for about six months. In the dream I was transported to the temple in South Korea where I had lived. I sensed a woman's voice guiding me, encouraging me to move deeper into the dream. I was aware of a nun offering divination to groups of Korean people in a way similar to my

Xhosa family. The lady's voice told me that this practice had been with humanity for eons. The nun's task was to feel the people who came to her for advice; to meditate, and from the depth of stillness offer up a few words of comfort or wisdom that could give them spiritual succor for the road ahead of them.

The lady then showed me a set of three cards with a strange design on the back. They looked like Zen tarot cards, but I had never seen anything like them before. A white light shimmered around them as snow swirled in the breeze of the South Korean winter.

When I woke, I felt the cold of the snow. I was also deeply humbled by the presence of "the lady" who had made me aware of the sacredness of my divining job and how similar it was to some older Korean spiritual practices. The three cards struck me; I sensed I was being shown a divining tool that would further unleash the wind inside me and bring me to deeper states of stillness that would help me serve my community and those seeking answers to some of life's difficult questions.

One night before sleeping, I meditated for about thirty minutes. No sooner had I closed my eyes than I felt a presence stirring in my room. I opened my eyes. Nothing. I closed them again and focused on my breathing. Then I saw an apparition in my mind's eye surrounded by light: it was a woman very much like Guanyin, a Buddhist saint, the bodhisattva of compassion and healing. Her voice captured my attention. She said, "Go to the Transkei." Then the woman spoke again, powerfully: "You need to go to the Transkei before you go to Ireland. *It is very important.*"

I had an image in my mind of where I had to go, a fifteen-hour drive to where some of my sangoma friends in the Pondo culture lived, near the forest and the sea. The next day I rushed to pack my things. I was jubilant, excited, and nervous. I was eager to meet Vuyo again, a sangoma teacher I had first met in a dream.

I felt comforted by my dream spirits on the long drive. I replayed my experiences in my mind while listening to the wind buffeting the car. The open road beckoned me forward like a muse from the sea promising to unfold the riches from the deep—spiritual wisdom like an intoxicating elixir to help me understand my life's calling.

Everything started to take on new meaning. The outer signs of life around me fed my inner world and encouraged me to keep going. The birds were flying in the right direction. The weather was calm. A feeling of peace buoyed me up and carried me safely toward my destination. My senses were heightened, and I didn't feel tired. The spirit of the lady from my dreams was with me constantly.

Vuyo greeted me with his characteristic warmth and good humor. His face was full of light and welcome. My spirit felt seen and at home despite the culture and language differences. He directed me to where I was to stay—the herbal hut where all the medicinal plants were prepared. Then we gathered in the main hut, a large circular room with a fire in the center where women and children were preparing the evening meal. There were happy smiles and an atmosphere of joy and togetherness. Everyone had a place in the community, and no one was excluded. The fire sizzled and seemed to be talking in a language I was unfamiliar with.

I was given a low stool in the form of an empty beer crate to sit on. Vuyo offered me some tea and homemade bread. I drank the tea, listened to the cheerful conversations around me, and watched the sun sink below the horizon across the valley. The tea and bread were delicious. My heart was singing, and I bowed down to the lady inside me, thanking her for bringing me to a place that felt like a homecoming.

I woke with the sun stretching across the mud floor and the sounds of birds and children's laughter in the air. The air was warm, with the lingering fragrance of herbs and cooking. After breakfast, Anathi, a good friend of Vuyo's, joined us. Anathi was a powerful trance dancer. It was said that when he danced the leopards came out of the forest to watch and connect with his spirit.

The three of us spent the day together like brothers, shooting the breeze. We visited the nearby town and then walked down to the sea, where Vuyo and Anathi taught me how to dance in the Pondo way. When I got the rhythm of it, I was astonished by the energy that was unleashed from my body. I felt exhilarated and as free as the seagulls flying close by. We smiled and laughed as we danced and danced. We danced for our ancestors, ourselves, our community, and for Africa—our home and all that we knew. Then, with the energy of the dance alive in our blood, we journeyed back to Vuyo's homestead.

Vuyo's wife, Mama, greeted us with a laugh and smile as we entered the homestead. She encouraged me to sit down. Then she said she had hidden my ceremonial sticks and I was to search for them with my spirit.

I was suddenly afraid, angry, and self-conscious. I felt very shy and didn't want to be tested in such a public way. But she encouraged me to pray and feel where my sticks were. This ancient sangoma training technique, to search for missing objects, is called *ukufihla*, and it is widely used in training diviners. My spirit was strong from the dancing, and now it had to be trained in ukufihla. It is believed that the easiest things to find are our own ceremonial objects because they contain a spark of our spirit and are connected to us.

The energy, or umoya, continued to build inside me. Then, like a dark cloud, it descended and smashed like thunder across the threshold of my world. I stood up and shouted and swore at everyone in the room and then ran to the herb room, my sanctuary.

As silence follows lightning, so my thunderous outburst was met with a pause and silence. Then people started chattering again, the children carried on running, and the dogs continued to search and sniff as I left the room.

I felt so embarrassed. My body was shaking. I am normally a very polite person, and I was shocked by my own behavior. After a few minutes, Vuyo appeared with a large tray of tea and homemade bread. I told him how sorry I was.

He smiled lovingly and said, "*Uyoyika qha!*" (You are just afraid!) Then he explained the umoya that rises inside us like a phoenix and helps us search for missing objects, as well as what is wrong with people: it is our own spirit that comes alive inside us and helps us to "divine," to see the soul of all things and connect with people and "see" what is happening to them.

After getting something solid in my body and sweet tea, I returned to my testing ground.

Mama greeted me again, looked into my eyes, and said, "*Khupha iintonga zakho!*" (Find your ceremonial sticks!) I was encouraged to say the first impulse or thought that came to mind but was thinking, *No way are they in that place.* I then went straight to my second thought. Mama went to look and said, "No, they are not there." She encouraged me to listen to my spirit and go with the quiet voice inside me, repeating that it is normally your first thought or image that reveals the hiding place. I listened carefully to her, felt my nervous tension again, prayed, and saw with my eyes closed the image of where the sticks were, lying next to a box of matches. I opened my eyes and told her.

"Yes," she said and went to collect them for me. I felt not just relief but awe at the sheer simplicity of the process.

My Western education was all about analyzing facts and coming up with a good argument that could be proven in reality. Divination training felt completely different—and refreshing. I didn't have to prove how clever I was but could be myself and allow my spirit to surface and shine. The scary part was allowing the deep, vulnerable part of me to speak. The adage "Through vulnerability comes strength" never felt more apt.

Vuyo and I went into the nearby village. I noticed that the vegetation surrounding it was lush, and the forest intruded from all directions. A local man joked that if he didn't cut the vines back, they would enter his house and in no time at all the jungle would reclaim his property like waves washing up a beach. I thought, *Civilization is as thin as the cracks in the wall through which the jungle enters.* I liked this idea, and it inspired me to keep going in pursuit of my own wilderness. For when we are completely wild, we connect to our intuition, and the Western mind filters—of always being correct, nice, and polite—no longer seem so important.

My spirit longed for the old Africa where we humans were a small part of nature and not the behemoth we are today. The village reminded me of that bygone time, and the wildness of my sangoma friends encouraged me to keep feeling, living, and dancing.

Vuyo and Anathi walked down the streets like kings, wearing white and blue beads around their necks and red and yellow bands across their foreheads. Their beads formed geometric shapes, waves and triangles, which only added to their nobility. Their spines were straight, and they walked with confidence and pride. It was wonderful to be in the presence of people who liked who they were and believed in themselves. This was the positive side of pride: to be able to enjoy your body and rejoice in your spirit and the gift of being alive.

We stopped at a café close to the sea surrounded by trees. It exuded a smell of fresh coffee. As I entered the café, my spine suddenly tingled and my breath caught in my chest. Straight in front of us was a round wooden table with a deck of tarot cards neatly placed in the center. The cards had the same design on their backs as in my dream. I had never seen them in reality. Until that moment I had thought my dream was just a dream.

As I sat down, Vuyo asked me if I knew how to work with cards. I said no but that I had dreamed these cards. He asked if I could give him a reading. I opened the pack—and there were the three cards from my dream.

The wind from the dream came rushing through me. I felt transported to the wisdom and clarity of my South Korean temple training. Looking at the cards, I spoke to Vuyo and divined the patterns in his life. He smiled, nodded, and said "Camagu!"

This stage of my vumisa training was now complete.

# PART V

## Initiation

# 11

# Call to Ireland

The years of my apprenticeship flew by like dreams in the wind. Family and friends asked me what I did in the township when I spent months at a time working with MaMngwevu. At first I didn't know what to say except that we worked with plants, people, ancestors, and dreams—a vague and esoteric answer. Finally, I made it simpler: "I spend time with my Xhosa elders, drinking tea and discussing life."

My mom and dad were very fond of MaMngwevu, Tat' uSukwini, and Tat' Bongani, a dignified man who helped me with the intricacies of the isiXhosa language and culture. My parents noticed that I was growing and maturing through my training. But after I had been a sangoma apprentice for more than eight years, my mom, exasperated, asked, "John, when will you finish your sangoma training? When will you become a full sangoma?"

"I don't know, Mom," I said.

This answer wasn't good enough for her. "Then go ask MaMngwevu."

So at my next elder meeting, I said my mother had a question for MaMngwevu. I explained that she was frustrated with the years going by and wondered when I would finish my apprenticeship. There was a short silence punctuated by big grins, shaking heads, and much laughter. Eventually, Mama said, "*Ixhomekeka kwizinyanya zakho.*" (It depends on your ancestors.) I would know I had finished when my ancestors told me in my dreams.

When I explained to my mother that it depended on our ancestors, she too was amused. "Knowing our lot, that could be forever."

I was happy to continue to serve my teacher as an apprentice as she served her community. But I also knew that this would pass and be followed by something bigger and even more challenging. I felt a myriad of emotions about my future sangoma road—from fear to nervous excitement. It felt like the job was much bigger than I was, and I hoped I had the strength to fulfill it. My elders' laughter and measured smiles gave me the confidence to keep walking.

## THE CALL OF THE "LITTLE PEOPLE" BACK TO IRELAND

In 1998, my mother and I traveled to Ireland to visit her family, and I took a break from my training. I hadn't seen the Irish countryside for twenty years, not since I was a small child, so as our plane descended approaching Dublin, I was amazed at how green everything was and how calm nature appeared, with soft undulating hills and hedges. I looked and felt like a wild man from distant shores, but I was ready to meet my relatives and reconnect with my Irish ancestors.

A few days after arriving, I dreamed about both the "little people" of Ireland and the ancestors of Tat' uSukwini's clan. The little people were a group of men with pointy green hats, beards, twinkly eyes, and an aura of laugher and mischief. They greeted me like a long-lost son. There was a sense of herbs about them, and I felt kinship with both the sea and the herbal realms. In the same dream, my adopted Xhosa ancestors—again, all men—also greeted me, wearing navy blue and white beads around their heads, the mark of elder men: *iinkosi*, headmen or chiefs. They reached their hands out to me and called me "*nyana*," son.

An abundance of Irish folktales center around the little people, or leprechauns, that appeared in my dream. Legend says they once openly inhabited Ireland before being pushed into the twilight worlds between the mundane, earthly realms and the spirit. These little people are seen in all cultures. In South Africa we have the *tikoloshe*. Some are playful and helpful while others are sinister and vindictive and look like goblins; like humans, the tikoloshe have the capacity for good and bad deeds. West African writer Malidoma Somé refers to the little people of his culture as the *gontomble*. They inhabit both this world and others and are keepers of herbal lore and natural wisdom. They are also the gatekeepers between the worlds, and people must give offerings and respect to them in order to be allowed to proceed into other spaces.[1] Little people in all cultures have important teachings for humanity in the form of stories that weave together humor, playfulness, tribal lore, and music. Their speech is said to have a rhythmic quality, as if they are mirroring nature in the form of the wind through the hedges or the tides of the sea.

I woke from my dream near Galway's harbor with the sea breeze on my face and the smell of seaweed lingering in the air. South Africa and Ireland were thousands of miles apart, and I seemed to exist in the barren wilderness and seascapes in between. My task was to marry my African and Irish spirits.

My mother soon returned to South Africa, but my dreams called me to stay. I would spend seven years in Ireland, leaving only to return for three- to four-month stretches to continue my sangoma training. My task in Ireland was to try to learn to feel comfortable in my Irish skin and come home to myself as an Afro-Celt healer—and to integrate my inner life with the world around me.

The charismatic, wandering drunkards on the streets of Galway constantly reminded me of this task. With their piercing stares and often musical voices, they demonstrated the world of the little people—the fairy world or the dreamtime. I became friends with a few of these characters, as did my artist friends, for they were an important part of Galway life. With their two feet in the liminal world of drunkenness and sometimes half a foot in the here and now, they reminded us all that the line between sanity and madness is very thin.

I lost myself in the Irish mist. I played my drum on the streets of Galway and befriended the town's musicians and street performers.

From the circus people, I learned how to juggle; from the charismatic street people, how to captivate audiences; and from the traditional Irish musicians, the magic of music. Life was exciting—I had never met young people who were so carefree, innocent, and happy. The burden and memory of apartheid, the South African civil war, and the poverty in the townships all began to recede. Ireland taught me about two of the most important medicines, humor and music.

I longed to live a normal life and to be Irish but my dreams took me to ancient Africa. And each time I woke up and returned from these nocturnal experiences, I felt a vacuum building inside me and a sense of desolation and despair over how to bring my gifts into the world.

Despite my desire to be Irish, my accent remained South African. And because of my white skin and blue eyes, my Irish and international friends couldn't absorb the fact that I was a sangoma. African music was the rage, and everyone I knew had a djembe (West African drum). But when I tried to explain that the rhythms were portals to the ancestral worlds, I was met with blank stares. My new friends gave me a reprieve from Africa, but I had to create new stories for myself in my new home that everyone could relate to. Africa was just too far away for them.

I was in Ireland to find out who I was, to connect with my blood. The Irish people reminded me of my adopted Xhosa community, richly expressing themselves in metaphor through poetry, literature, and music. This was the language of dreams and mysticism, the language I was most accustomed to.

The Irish landscape was calling me to go deeper into my bones, into the wind and fabric of my being. I felt called to go on pilgrimage to Croagh Patrick, the holiest mountain in Ireland. Legend has it that this was the place where Saint Patrick drove the snakes out of Ireland, marking the beginning of Ireland's move from a traditional pagan or druidic spirituality to Catholicism.[2]

As a sangoma apprentice, I had numerous dreams about snakes. During my time in Ireland, I dreamed of little snakes living beneath the soil, holding the fabric of life together. I decided to climb Croagh Patrick to understand my own calling and to praise the ancient spirit of Ireland and the holy man Saint Patrick. Perhaps he had instead *honored* the mountain's snakes, the symbol of healing and transformation, and banished ignorance, pride, and resentment, the true "snakes" or hindrances, to human transformation.

The night before my climb, I dreamed of an ancient castle on top of a mountain. It looked like a skeleton, its walls down. There were numerous stone archways leading into rooms with no walls. A wind blew through the castle as I was led to deeper places within it. A powerful woman with long flowing gray hair guided me from one room to the next. She had the aura of a goddess, and I felt fear and excitement as we went deeper into the castle.

She pointed to a strange, bonelike object in the heart of the castle. The object filled me with awe and an ancient, almost primal fear. I felt ready to journey further into my spirit and understand the mystery of my Irish ancestral past.

My friend Seamus and I journeyed to Croagh Patrick on Reek Sunday, the annual day of pilgrimage to the mountain. Up to forty thousand people make the climb each year, on the last Sunday in July.[3]

As we arrived at the foot of the holy mountain on this auspicious day, I marveled to see the elderly, the blind, and people with serious physical complaints braving the mountain with a stoic spirit, filled with laughter and optimism and surrounded by family and friends to lend support. This was about more than the individual; it was about the community, the family, and helping one another. It was an Irish equivalent of Ubuntu.

I was in relatively good shape but found the climb quite difficult. It was very steep, and the shale rock near the top was tricky to navigate. But the view was spectacular. I could see far out to sea, as well as green hills and valleys in all directions. With each step, I felt the spirit of the mountain.

I went to a special place near the top and burned some impepho from South Africa. I placed some tobacco on top to honor my ancestors and a bit of camphor to honor the Great Spirit and gods of the land. I asked to connect more deeply to my Irish roots and to complete my sangoma calling.

People up and down the mountain were praying, laughing, and singing. Croagh Patrick became a symbol of repentance, humility, prayer, humanity, and, above all, honoring the ancient spirit of our forefathers and mothers, represented by the bonelike object in my dream. The spirit of my ancestors transmuted time, space, and the outward manifestations of religion and spiritual practice, which, like the wind, is always changing. Our work is always to find the bone of truth within life.

No matter how fit, young, or healthy a person was, the mountain could make you feel small. We were stripped bare to our basic humanity. Each arduous step up was an exercise in letting go of attachments such as ego, pride, and resentment. And each step down was an expression of joy in being alive.

The mountain taught me about my own vulnerability. The only thing I could share was my own breath, the wind or spirit of life inside me. This I had offered up in my prayers at the top. My pilgrimage was almost over.

I met an old friend, Jose, a well-known Galway alcoholic who spent time in various homeless shelters. He told me he was climbing the mountain to honor a much-loved friend of his, Michael, who had died over the weekend, found dead in a pub in Dublin with a needle in his arm.

Jose spoke quietly to me with his head bowed low. "Jesus, Michael was a lovely man, John. He just hurt so much. We all tried to help him. There was nothing we could do for him in the end. At least now his pain is over. I am here for him, to say good-bye."

I was greatly humbled by Jose's act of brotherly love. Many sensitive souls are lost to drug overdose or suicide in Ireland. In my own small circle of friends, we lost one too, also a gentle soul who struggled with the pain of life and ended up taking his.

One of my earliest memories of Ireland is of riding on the shoulders of one of my relatives, Aedan, when I was six. Twenty years later, Aedan welcomed me back to his home, where he opened up the world of the little people to me and inspired me with Irish folklore. He was also prone to the "good stuff" and likened Guinness to petrol, fuel that gave him the energy to get through the day. He could really "see" people and had a charismatic common touch about him, making anyone feel at ease in his company. One day when I was sitting with him, he said, "You are a very tormented young man. You should try Guinness—it will sort you out." He could see my shamanic calling and the illness we call the thwasa. But fortunately, I never followed his advice.

Aedan's words, rang like a bell through my spirit, while my prayers on Croagh Patrick sped up my sangoma calling in an unexpected and frightening way. I longed for my home in South Africa. I slipped into a deep depression. I saw my own illness mirrored in the faces of my homeless friends and addicts. I felt empty and lost inside. A darkness appeared around my eyes, and I was being pulled to faraway places. It became harder for me to ground myself. I knew I had to resume my apprenticeship, for therein lay the medicine for my soul. Yet during this period of my life in Ireland, I didn't reach out to MaMngwevu. I felt ashamed because I didn't have enough money to return home.

One night I awoke suddenly and bolted upright. I was gasping for breath, and all I could say was "*Uxolo, Mama, uxolo!*" (I am sorry, Mother, I am sorry!) In my dream, MaMngwevu and Tat' uSukwini approached me. I was kneeling on the ground and they reached down to me to shake my hand, saying only, "*Uphi, Cingo? Uphi?* (Where are you, John? Where are you?) I felt a bolt of electricity flood through me and was aware of a light surrounding us. I was being called back home to complete my apprenticeship with MaMngwevu.

I felt guilty that I had not been in touch with her. A few days later I phoned home and spoke to MaMngwevu's son, Zongezile. I told him my situation and apologized for not being in touch. He said his parents were very worried about me. Later I heard that MaMngwevu had done a special prayer to uThixo to ask whether I was alive or dead.

My spirit felt better after I made contact with my teacher, and my energy levels started to improve. But I still had a major problem: I didn't have the money to return home.

Again, I woke up from one of my dreams. I was with MaMngwevu, and there was white light all around us. She asked me what was wrong—why was I scraping my feet about returning home? I explained to her that I still had no money. She looked at me and clicked a few times, shaking her head as if money was not a good enough excuse. Then she stood up and said, "*Uyoyika! Ndiza kuthetha no Thixo!*" (You are afraid! I am going to speak to the Great Spirit!) And with that she turned suddenly and moved off toward a tunnel of white light.

A number of things happened after that. Life moved at lightning speed, and doors opened. Many people assisted me in surprising ways. I befriended a traditional medicine man from North America who gave me some wonderful advice. As we prayed together in the countryside outside Galway, he said, "Son, don't pray for money! Just pray that the ways will be opened for you. If you pray for money you will only limit how Spirit can help you."

I took his advice. I prayed near the sea, in the valleys, and around the rivers. I sprinkled tobacco near and far. A mere three weeks later, I returned home to South Africa.

# 12

# Back to Africa

## Umgoduso (Final Initiation), Dreams, and Signs

I felt part of something greater, and overwhelmed with gratitude, as I touched down in Johannesburg. I was greeted by the smells of African plants, the sounds of thunder and lightning, and the smiling, jovial atmosphere of the local people. I was home, and my heart was at peace. Another adventure was about to start, and I felt buoyed up by a hidden force.

Within the first few weeks of returning home, I received the dream I had been waiting for. Before I went to sleep, I had meditated and then went outside to gaze at the stars. They were shining brightly, with a magic and energetic pull all of their own.

In my dream, a wild ox came searching for me. It appeared "otherworldly," simultaneously innocent and supernaturally strong. Intense white light permeated the entire dream—it was almost like looking directly at the sun. Part of me felt afraid, but the animal's wild innocence also carried the invitation of an unusual relationship that I couldn't quite yet understand.

When I awoke, I was happy. I felt sure this was my final dream, that my ancestors had spoken through the ox and my sangoma apprenticeship was over. But like all my sangoma dreams, I had to discuss it with my teacher for validation.

About a month later, I returned to my teacher's home in the heart of the Eastern Cape. As I drove my old VW over the weather-beaten dirt road of the township, I waved to passers-by who called out to me:

"*Molo, Cingo*" (Hello, John) or "Camagu!" Rain had just fallen and the dirt roads were muddy and slow. I could smell the loamy quality of the soil as the sun beat down. Little children waved to me from the side of the road, shouting, "Cingo, Cingo!"

I was anxious about how I would be received after being gone for so long (almost two years), but my elders treated me just as before, with a lighthearted ease, as if I had just left the room for a moment. They admonished me gently for being out of touch, and I promised I would always communicate in the future. The atmosphere in Mama and Tata's house was the same as always; it radiated a palpable feeling of love and togetherness.

I described my dream to MaMngwevu, the ox looking for me, and my feeling of fear. She laughed and cried out, "*Inkomo yakho!*" (That is your ox!) She smiled sweetly and turned to her husband, and they both nodded approvingly, saying, "*Ugqibile ukuthwasa! Uyaphuma ngoku. Uyagoduka.*" (You've finished your training! You are getting out now! You are going home!) I had finished my training and they would now take me home to my family (which she meant metaphorically, mystically, and literally).

Mama and Tata explained that first we needed to work on the closing initiation ceremonies, which would last a full week. Mama described a few things we would need and said they were difficult to obtain and required a lot of preparation. First, I had to find my ox; it would be sacrificed on the final day of my initiation. She knew a few farmers I could speak to. My mind was a whirlwind of questions, and in true sangoma Zen style I was forced to be patient and trust in my elders and these ancient rites of passage.

Part of me was sad to say good-bye to my youth and my time as an apprentice, and I was nervous about stepping more fully into my destiny as a sangoma. I felt the wind of transformation building inside me. I respectfully thanked my teacher and surrendered to the next stage of my journey.

I settled into a daily practice of drinking and washing with plant medicines, Mama's usual mix of about five medicinal plants from the nearby grasslands and forests. The herbs had a wonderful, rich aroma, sweet and earthy. When I bathed in the herbal mixture, I entered deeper states of consciousness and felt a sense of peace and harmony flowing through me, which expressed itself in my dreams at night.

Then I added to my bathing mix a powerful plant used to remove curses, one I had seen in a dream. The plant, which oozed a sticky liquid that was very itchy, was growing in my friend's garden. After performing a blessing and asking the Great Spirit for permission, I cut a few thin strips of the bulb of the plant and added it to my herbal washing mix.

In the bath that night I felt like an electric current had switched on. I had added too much to the mixture. My whole body was on fire with itching. My heart rate soared to over 150 beats a minute. I tried to stay in the bath with the mantra "This is good for you. This is good for you." But eventually I couldn't take it any longer—my skin felt so hot and itchy that I jumped out of the bath and ran naked around the house to cool off. Eventually, the itchiness subsided to a low tingle and my whole body felt alive as my heartbeat pulsed like a flickering blue flame.

I was pleased by this reaction, despite the severity. I was preparing myself to become a full igqirha, a Khoisan word meaning "the one who holds the lightning rod of the ancestors." My nervous system had to be able to absorb a high level of energy. To do this adequately, I had to cleanse my body.

I was rewarded that night with a dream of Khoisan-looking people, dancing in a cave. Their bodies were moving in sync in a spiral, like a long snake. The earth shook, and I was left with the vibrational feeling of the oneness of man, that we are all one human family moving together, however discordant we may sometimes appear.

I had been transported to a timeless, mystical world. In Gaelic, the ancient and traditional language of Ireland, this world is called Tir na Nog, the place of everlasting youth. For me it is the dreamtime, which I believe exists as a parallel universe to our own time. The more we connect to our own spirit, the more we can connect to that part of us that lives in the dreamtime, the part of us that is immortal and perpetually changing and growing, becoming more connected to uThixo.

When I spoke to Mama the next day she said the dream was a good sign. I was connecting to the timeless world of my ancestors. This would continue to happen until the final initiation. The rhythm of these ancient voices mixed with my own. It felt like my blood, or DNA, was pulsing to a timeless beat, and an integral part of me was waking up.

In tracking my dreams, I noticed a mystical pattern involving the number three. This spilled over into my waking life, drawing my awareness to important omens, or signs, appearing in clusters of three, one after the other. One day I noticed one of my special medicine plants flowering, I heard the call of a rare sunbird, and there was a crab waiting on the threshold of my front door. It was unusual to see a crab, the symbol of the abantu bomlambo, so far from the water. I felt blessed by the natural world and my ancestral spirits residing within her, and I was looking forward to my final initiation.

The preparations commenced for my week of ceremony. I sat down with my elders in MaMngwevu's consulting room and made notes about everything we would need for the ceremony. Tata's clan included numerous elders who would all come to witness this historic occasion for South Africa and the Eastern Cape, as well as for our community. He said as far as he and the other elders were aware, I was the first white person in recent history (thirty or forty years) to finish the Xhosa sangoma training and receive the honorable title of igqirha elikhulu (literally translated as "big, or senior, sangoma").

In this traditional culture, great emphasis is placed on witnessing important occasions. The more people who can witness an important event, the greater the likelihood it will be remembered for future generations. A sangoma graduation ceremony needs to be seen by as many people as possible to celebrate both the medicine person's connection to the ancestral world and the community who assisted in their training. Sangoma training is recognized as extremely difficult—many people start it, yet only a handful complete it—and thus warrants a huge celebration when one of the community members gets this far. The sangoma family (including the sangoma initiate's blood family) is considered blessed because one of them is now seen to be a direct channel to the ancestral world.

To welcome the elder dignitaries, we needed copious amounts of brandy, beer, and gin. About five cases of brandy (twelve bottles per case) would be used to open and close the kraal space. Alcohol served the function of blessing the ceremony by inviting the ancestors of both our families to attend. We would honor my mother's people, the Kellys from Ireland; my father's people, the Lockleys, originally from England; and we would also honor the Ngwevus and the Sukwinis, as I was an adopted member of MaMngwevu's family.

Nelson Mandela's powerful legacy and his long walk to freedom resulted in the fall of apartheid. This in turn opened the door for my apprenticeship, making it possible for me to undergo sangoma training. And the fact that I, as a white man, and my European family were about to be honored by my adopted black Xhosa community was a testament to how far South Africa had come in terms of healing racial tension and recognizing one another for our own intrinsic humanity. I felt proud of my community and deeply humbled and grateful that so much effort was being expended to celebrate me and my family.

As my final initiation approached, my elders and I watched nature and our dreams for signs, listening and observing our inner and outer worlds for messages from the ancestral/spirit realm that would indicate how I was to use my gifts. The elders would create a safe harbor for my spirit to return home, to the source of life—and I would not return alone. I would be joined by the izinyanya, an army of spiritual warriors from the ancestral world. The elders would call on them from all the habitats of man: forest, cave, mountain, river, and sea—the sea being one of the most powerful dwelling places of our nature spirits.

## ANIMAL SACRIFICE

In the early years of my apprenticeship, I didn't question the sacrifice of animals; I naïvely thought that I might not have to do it. As a practicing Buddhist, I had done my best to maintain one of our most fundamental precepts: "Do not kill." But Zen Master Su Bong said that the most important thing about the Zen precepts was to follow the situation. If you broke the precept by not lying in order to protect life, for instance, that was considered correct. Even the taking of life needed to be observed according to the situation. These thoughts went through my head as my initiation day loomed.

During this time I had a number of strong dreams that helped guide and prepare me. One powerful dream helped clarify my thoughts and concerns about the coming ceremonial sacrifice. I saw a huge whirlpool of water or energy spiraling downward, feeding a point of energy in the center. Sacrificial animals stood on the outskirts of the whirlpool. A young goat got caught and disappeared into the center. I also saw a lion cub, a leopard, a tiger, and other wild animals that we sangomas honor. When I awoke, I understood the meaning behind animal sacrifice. The animals were being offered to the circle of life so we all could live more conscious lives.

Blood is extraordinarily sacred in the sangoma world because it keeps us alive and is a direct channel to our ancestors. It goes through our bones, which are a living reminder of our people and where we come from. After I told MaMngwevu my dream, she nodded in confirmation and said that we would need to sacrifice a goat a few days before my ox to let the ancestors know that my elders were preparing to take me home. To call the ancestors and ask for their blessing, we would need to give them the blood of life. In many cases in the Xhosa tradition, this comes in the form of the humble goat.

In the Bushmen, or Khoisan, spiritual culture, when a sacred dream or omen necessitated the spilling of blood, they sacrificed a goat or sheep. If it was a goat, the people went to a group of goats and spoke to them with respect and reverence, saying, "Friends, we need one of you to be a messenger to our ancestors, to tell them that we send our greetings and our love. Can one of you be our messenger?" Then they would call the herd away and one goat would remain—the messenger given the sacred job of helping the people connect to their ancestors. I was always struck by the beauty and simplicity of this story.

I had the good fortune of experiencing this story when Tat' uSukwini and I visited a local farm. Tata told the farmer that we were looking for a goat for my upcoming ceremony, preferably a fat one because we were expecting many people. He replied, *"Ewe, sinayo ibhokhwe ityebile"* (Yes, we have fat goats), and shouted to a young goat herder, asking him to please bring all the goats into the nearby field. As is customary, we were looking for a young male. We also sought the best-looking white-coated goat, white being the color of uThixo and our ancestors. We watched the goats for a few minutes, quietly taking in everything about them. Ideally we also wanted a "wild" one, a creature with high life-force energy, as they are known to make the best messengers. It is said that when they die, they carry our prayers on their backs into the spirit world.

The boy whistled and called the herd away. One goat remained, standing still and looking directly at us. He was large, with a quick temperament, a beautiful white coat, and a few ruddy brown markings down his side. Tata looked at me and pulled on his cigarette, inhaling in a meditative way, and then said, "*Cingo, ibhokwe yakho. Ityebile kakhulu. Iyakuthanda!*" (John, that is your goat. He is very fat. He likes you!) Tata smiled wistfully, giggled like a little boy, and made a joke. We all laughed affectionately together—even the goat seemed to smile and nod his head while we enjoyed Tata's charismatic way.

It was time to take the goat back to MaMngwevu's house. The men shouted, "Camagu!" and tied the goat's legs together to transport it home. This time the goat gave a piercing cry, shaking our spirits and alerting a nearby flock of birds. The men again shouted, "Camagu!" The goat's behavior was showing us that the ancestors were happy and that we had chosen the correct goat.

Tat' uSukwini is often called on by the Sukwini clan to sacrifice goats and oxen for their ancestors. Despite occasional ill health and old age, he proudly dons his white and turquoise head beads more weekends than he can count. His job is a sacred one, and in a similar way to the sangoma calling, he received dreams from his ancestors calling him to don the beads and wield the knife to dispatch the animals over the waters to the ancestral realm.

Tata described his calling as involving an apprenticeship like mine; the older men in the clan passed on their gifts to him. His job is a difficult one, requiring resolve and a steady hand. The animals panic and he calms them. I have seen him calm all kinds of animals, from wild township dogs to goats and oxen; I liken him to an animal whisperer.

## SEARCHING FOR THE OX

My initiation ceremony was about two weeks away, and my ox was calling. A contingent of elders and I went through the countryside looking at cattle. A few brief forays yielded no results except sunburn and a chance to laugh again with the elder men. Then Tata suggested that we contact a well-known cattle breeder in the area. Tata phoned him and quickly described the kind of ox we were looking for. The farmer said he had one similar to our description.

The next day we drove into the countryside. Arriving at the farm, we got out to stretch our legs. The sky was blue with a smattering of clouds. We heard cattle lowing in the distance. The whiff of Tata's cigarette smoke signaled to the ancestors that we were looking for my dream ox. Suddenly an ox broke through the line of thick bushes in front of us, quickly followed by four more. The first ox ran toward us and then off to one side. He appeared exactly as I had dreamed him, and his horns were identical. "That's him!" I shouted.

We all shouted at the same time as we observed the simple symmetry and beauty of these large animals running through the African bushveld. Tata told me my ox was the "lead" ox, as it guided the others through the bush. I felt as though I had returned to the days when simple rituals like this were a part of life. I felt the dreamtime descending upon me as my dream collided with my life. My spirit was now ready to return home.

My ceremony began in the traditional African way—and the Celtic way, for that matter—with the brewing of beer, the traditional *umqombothi*, about four days before the ceremony. It is a heady mix of maize (corn), maize malt, sorghum malt, yeast, and water.[1] Brewing is an art form that is handed down from one generation to the next. The beer is brewed over an open fire outside the home, with prayers uttered throughout the brewing. Making, drinking, and offering beer are ways for everyone to connect to the ancestral world and one another.

My umqombothi was almost ready when my ox was delivered about a week later. He arrived like an explosion. The opening ceremony was about to start, but the farmer was late. We can often gauge the power of a particular ceremony by the amount of chaos or discordant energy involved before it starts, and I had to keep reminding myself of this while we waited. Then we heard shouts coming from the street. Apparently the truck carrying the ox was stuck in another part of the township. My ox was bellowing and had attracted all the local cattle, who rushed toward it, creating a traffic jam. We could hear the ruckus from a kilometer away, and we went to find out what was happening. Tata, the animal whisperer, talked to it while other elders led the local cattle away.

Finally, my ox had arrived! As soon as it entered Tat' uSukwini's kraal, it kicked up a storm and broke the tree that stood in the center. There was a cacophony of sounds: men shouting, dust whirling, goats and children running, cattle bellowing in support. Tata quietly entered the kraal and tossed a rope over the ox's back. His expression was steely,

Roman, the sacrificial ox.

but underneath it was limitless compassion, for he felt the animal's fear and moved quickly to calm it down. Tata's son, Zongezile, joined him and talked to the ox, calling him Roman—meaning "red man" in English—because he had a beautiful red coat. According to Xhosa custom, we must name the ceremonial ox so its spirit can feel at home and connect to the people.

When Tat' uSukwini spoke to Roman and called him by his new name, the ox calmed down. I was amazed. The large beast and small man together were a sight to behold. Tata brought it some water and it bellowed in response. Everyone shouted, "Camagu!" praising the spirits of nature and our ancestors. Joyful Christians might shout "Amen!" or "Blessed be!" to convey a similar feeling of awe in the presence of something sacred.

The elders and I went inside and prepared ourselves with ceremonial clothes and beads to welcome Roman to the Sukwini kraal. Tata stood with his stick and fabric thrown over his left shoulder and called in all his ancestors. He announced this was the start of the *umgoduso* (homecoming) ceremony for uCingolweendaba (John Lockley), and he welcomed in the Kellys, Lockleys, and all the ancestors related to me, saying they were very welcome in the Sukwini home. He then welcomed in his own ancestors and MaMngwevu's and said we were all gathered together to welcome the ceremonial ox we called Roman.

We walked out to the kraal in single file with Tat' uSukwini leading, followed by me, MaMngwevu, and the other elders. The sun was setting. Cattle bellowed, birds sang, and stray township dogs ran in all directions. People stopped to look over the hedge at this huge ox that dominated the kraal. The ground shook as he pounded the earth, celebrating our entrance to the kraal. Tata blessed the kraal space, pouring a sprinkle of brandy on the entrance, then on the ixhanti in the center and a small space at the back representing the forest spirits. He beseeched his ancestors to assist us and bless this ceremony, telling them we were gathered for my umgoduso, and he welcomed Roman.

Then MaMngwevu spoke. Her voice rose to a crescendo as she chanted the names of her ancestors, the sound matching the bellowing ox and reaching to the heavens. She was in a state of rapture as she spoke about my calling and how I had entered her home. She declared I was like one of her own children and had shown nothing but love and respect for her and her family. She asked all the ancestors to bless me and accept me into the world of being an igqirha elikhulu. Then, like a calm after a storm, she sat down. I was encouraged to speak.

Speaking in isiXhosa, I thanked my ancestors and the Great Spirit for bringing me to the Sukwini clan and teaching me the old ways. I praised Tat' uSukwini and MaMngwevu for their love and support. I also praised my own parents. I asked the ancestors to open the way and bless my ceremony. I also praised Roman and asked the great ones to bless him as he traveled to the other world for me.

The elder men stood in turn and thanked me for being with them and having the courage to stick with my apprenticeship through many years of training. Their words were like a stream of sweet water, easing my soul after all the difficulties I had experienced. In that moment, everything seemed worth it. I felt so lucky, privileged, and blessed. The impepho smoke mixed with tobacco and rose in the breeze as we all watched. MaMngwevu poked me in the ribs and pointed to a flock of three ducks flying overhead. While the last elder spoke, a little wagtail bird sat close by singing sweetly, seeming to be part of the conversation. The birds were considered ancestral birds, umoya wezilo (animal spirits), and were honored guests at any ceremony. MaMngwevu smiled and the elders exclaimed together, "Camagu!" The signs were good; it was going to be a powerful ceremony—something none of us would ever forget.

My seven-day ceremony had begun. We went back to the house, where the elders carried on speaking and debating for hours. More joined us. The house hummed to a forgotten tune—the ancestors were waking up. I felt my spirit moving toward the harbor. My guardian spirits hovered in the distance, waiting, watching. Roman stood guard. And the sun sank below the horizon. I sensed electricity in the air: something was about to happen.

The elders told me my ox was particularly large and its spirit was strong. I felt in my heart the importance of doing this sacrifice, but I also felt very sad that this beautiful animal had to die for me. But now I was a

Xhosa sangoma medicine man, an igqirha, and Roman's sacrifice would strengthen me and heal my spirit. To have the sickness of being called by the ancestral spirits is a powerful and delicate thing. We have to continually look for ways to ground our spirit in the material, earthly world. The blood sacrifice of Roman would aid this process.

I went over to Roman to speak to him. He was stomping on the ground, and I could hear his deep, deliberate breaths. My heart ached with gratitude and appreciation for the sacrifice he was about to make. I thanked him for joining us and being our ancestral messenger. I told him I was sorry that he had to die, but that we honored him and he must not linger in this world but go directly to the other side. I asked him to please tell my ancestors that I honored them as well and that I accepted my calling to become an igqirha elikhulu. I asked him to thank them for choosing me. And I prayed that I would do good work in this world and the next. Roman just moved from side to side while I spoke to him. I looked into his eyes. They were the eyes of pure innocence and love, like all animals I've connected with. He was joined by a few of Tata's cows to help calm him down and by my sacrificial goat, whose white coat shimmered in the moonlight. I spoke briefly to him too, thanking him for his sacrifice.

The mindful sacrifice of animals, though hard, has a bittersweet edge. I have observed their spirits feeding the ground and nourishing the people's hearts in all directions. I have also observed an abundance of dreams afterward. When done correctly with prayers of honor and gratitude, the animal's blood feeds the source of life, the source of the whirlpool energy in my dreams. In one of my dreams I saw a multitude of people, friends, and family joined together in an intricate web through the blood of the ox. I saw the upcoming ceremony drawing us closer together as human beings, as well as closer to the plant and animal worlds.

The pulse of the drum could be felt in the earth as the amagqirha began to raise the energy for the sacrificial ceremony. MaMngwevu's apprentices had arrived to support me, to sing, drum, and raise the ancestral energy of the home so we could connect with the other side. They were beautifully dressed in white cloth with embroidered designs and colorful beads. Their entire faces were painted white in the custom of apprenticing Xhosa sangomas, though a few of the senior apprentices had white only around their eyes. They seemed otherworldly as they arrived in the home, as if from the sea or the mist of the ancestral world, and greeted MaMngwevu in a respectful way on their knees. They then greeted in turn each of the elders in the home. Everyone moved to an unwritten script accompanied by laughter and storytelling as they moved into the back rooms with large bags of beads and blankets. This space was the training ground for new apprentices to learn and older ones to instruct. It was an opportunity for the community to get reacquainted, for new relationships to be forged and old ones rekindled. This would be my home for the next seven days.

Iingoma were played throughout the night, interspersed with sangomas dancing in the center of the room and shouting "Pheza!" (Stop!) as they felt their spirits rising within them. Then they prayed and honored their ancestors and asked for a blessing on the upcoming ceremony. In the small space, only two or three people could dance at a time. The rest of us clapped our hands and sang our hearts out.

The next day we woke before the rising sun. We performed our morning ablutions, washing ourselves meticulously and putting on our ceremonial clothes. We were preparing to talk to the ancient ones on behalf of our communities, to be spiritual messengers. For me, old wounds, cracks in the psyche, and fragility surfaced, something I had felt many times before. My own pain and vulnerability burned inside. My hands shook as I put on my beads, and my stomach was in knots. I felt like I was stepping out onto a narrow ledge with an infinite drop beneath me.

The sangoma path is the way of the "wounded healer." We have to feel our pain and vulnerability in order to be open vessels and receive the wisdom and guidance of the izinyanya. My spirits were dismantling me in order for me to be more open inside.

We all gathered in the house, a sight to behold, looking like the nature spirits we were about to pray to. We shone with dignity, grace, and a special kind of electricity as we waited in silence for our elders to lead us. Tat' uSukwini told us we would all go to pray to the sea, river, and forest; to call on our ancestors to bless us and bless my sacrificial ceremony.

Then Mama, Tata, and several elders and initiates all piled into a few waiting cars, with Mama and Tata joining me as I drove the lead car. Mama placed her sacred sticks on the dashboard, I placed mine next to hers, and off we went into the wilderness around us. We drove in silence, watching for signs and listening to our dreams, divining nature to track omens, blessings, and messages from the izinyanya.

## NATURE AS DIVINATION — TRACKING NATURE, TRACKING SPIRIT

The sun crested the horizon as mist rose from the wet road, creating a mysterious haze. The countryside around us consisted of thick bush interspersed with open grassland. Occasionally, MaMngwevu pointed to a plant and mentioned its qualities. As we descended a steep ravine, a troop of baboons crossed the road. We all shouted "Camagu!" and honored and praised our ancestors.

The baboon (*imfene* in isiXhosa) is one of my animal spirits (*isilo*), something I discovered after a number of mysterious dreams and physical encounters. Many sangomas have baboon isilo. This animal is one of the guardians of the plant world, and when they come to us in a dream it is considered very lucky. They are the "old men of the bushveld" that depart their intuitive wisdom to us sangomas so we can maintain the balance between the natural world and man. A large alpha baboon stood guard over the troop. My friends laughed and pointed at it, as they felt it represented me and my upcoming ceremony: a lucky omen.

We rounded another bend and roared, "Camagu!" This time a troop of monkeys—renowned as an isilo of the Ngwevu clan—was crossing the road. This was a sign that the Ngwevu ancestors were with us. Our animal totems help open the road for us, enabling us to fulfill our life purpose. They are a sign from our ancestral spirits that we are not alone and that our lives are blessed and supported by them. The physical road we were traveling represented our spiritual road, and our earlier prayers had primed the ancestors to direct and guide us. These signs of nature were also indications of how the ancestors wanted me to use my sangoma gifts in the world.

We arrived at the sea as the sun broke through the clouds and spread its inviting rays across the ocean surface. MaMngwevu stormed toward the sea like a general leading her troops into battle. The ancestors were waiting, and she was anxious to start her prayers before the sun climbed any higher. I grabbed her ceremonial sticks and ran after her. We all greeted the ducks flying overhead with "Camagu!" and waited for MaMngwevu to open the morning prayers.

The water lapped gently at our feet as our white garments flapped in the wind. It was cold. We watched the sea for signs. Then Mama began, shouting amid the roaring sea and whistling wind: "*Camagu bantu abadala. Ndiqula; izinyanya zam.*" (I honor and praise you old people. I honor and praise my ancestors.) When she paused, we all responded to her prayers with "Camagu!" Mama made offerings of tobacco, rose petals, and an assortment of herbs to the sea.

As MaMngwevu prayed and chanted, the sea seemed to rise up and take on a life of its own. It became a living, breathing creature, with the power to grant our wishes or take our lives. We stepped gingerly on the cloak of her white foam with a sense of trepidation and excitement.

So MaMngwevu opened her heart and prayed like her life depended on it. She prayed to her ancestors, the Great Spirit, and the spirits of the sea. She asked them to bless her family and bless my sangoma umgoduso ceremony. She scattered white and turquoise beads into the waves while chanting her prayers in a quick, staccato fashion.

The sea responded by moving closer to her. Suddenly she was drenched above her knees. Apprentices rushed to her side, holding her elbows from both sides and pulling her back from the sea, but she was in another world, and the fingers of the sea were drawing her closer. Another wave rushed toward her as she finished her prayers. At the same time, the elder men and sangomas started talking and pointing to the horizon. In a reef out to sea, there appeared a carriage of light that moved across the water. Tata pointed and whispered, "*Abantu bomlambo bapendula thina.*" (The spirits from the sea have answered our prayers.) We all screamed, "Camagu!"

Then nature herself began talking to us—from the earth, wind, and sky. Flocks of ducks and seagulls called in their flight above us—"Aiaaaikkkkk! Aiaaaaikkkk! Aaiikk!"—and we replied, "Camagu, Camagu!" The sea crept toward us with a rhythm of its own and whirlpools of water appeared beside us. All around us on the wet sand we suddenly saw sea snails that had burrowed and crawled in their language of spirals. And we all shouted our joy and love at being heard by the ancient ones: "Camagu!"

One by one we approached the sea to pray and make offerings to the sea spirits to ask their blessing. MaMngwevu completed the ritual by blowing her whistle and thanking the izinyanya for hearing our prayers and responding so well. Then we turned as one and moved up the beach, collecting sand and seawater. The prayers felt like a divine orchestral performance of music, rhythm, and light, with MaMngwevu as the conductor.

We drove back to the township. En route we stopped at a small sacred lake that had been frequented by the Xhosa people for generations. Again, Mama approached the water and addressed the abantu bomlambo, people of the river. Mama sprinkled some tobacco on the water and then threw a large handful into the center of the lake. It sank straight down and was followed by a series of bubbles that rose like Morse code from the depths of the water kingdom. The sangomas were ecstatic and shouted out, "Camagu!"

Mama stepped back from the water's edge and gave us a chance to pray to the waters of the lake. Each person received different messages, depending on where they were in their life. In the pauses between our prayers, stillness descended on the lake, as if the spirits were waiting for us. Then the magical interplay of animals, plants, and insects continued as we prayed from our hearts and directed our spirits to the heart of the lake. The lake became a divining mirror, reflecting our souls' journeys and offering us both a blessing and inspiration for the road ahead.

Once again, Mama closed the prayers with a few words to the waters. I sneaked back and dipped one of my sacred sticks in the water. I felt a bolt of electricity shoot through my stick and into me. This left me feeling quite jumpy, and I later apologized to Mama for breaking what felt like sacred protocol. She laughed and said I was afraid of the river people, who had power and magic aplenty. Then we both laughed, and Mama said everything was okay—I shouldn't worry.

MaMkhwemte, one of MaMngwevu's closest friends—a powerful woman with beady eyes, a dignified posture, and a welcoming smile—joined us in our car. She was an expert at harvesting medicinal plants, and as we drove through the countryside she pointed to unusual plants along the side of the road. At a special place alongside the road we stopped, climbed out, and walked up a hill to pray. MaMkhwemte asked the elder men to gather a few of the rare plants so she could use them for medicinal mixtures for clients. We walked toward an acacia tree with thorny bushes that seemed to tug at us, like a mysterious force trying to communicate in another language. Suddenly MaMkhwemte pointed at the tree, whispering in my ear and pulling on my arm. Following her gesture I saw a wildcat sitting on one of the branches, a bit smaller than a lynx or caracal and with beautiful spotted markings. How auspicious that the cat was sitting in the very tree we were going to use to direct our prayers to the forest kingdom, the last of our ancestral habitats. As we approached, it appeared to wait for us. Then it discreetly moved away.

MaMkhwemte told me this was a lucky sign from the forest people. They were blessing my journey and upcoming sacrificial ceremony.

After we finished our prayers, we were all exhausted, but our drive back home was filled with excited chatter. Our morning of ritual had been a huge success. Our ancestral and nature spirits had accepted my upcoming ceremony: the signs were clear that I was being blessed. All we had to do now was turn up, be present to the ceremony, and continue to honor our ancestors and uThixo.

We returned home to the sound of the drum. The amagqirha were waiting for us, singing one of my favorite iingoma, which speaks about the crab as the messenger from the river people. I reveled in the rhythms.

We waited for the elder men and sangomas to gather. Then Tat' uSukwini told of our journey to the sea, river, and forest, describing the amazing things we had witnessed. One of MaMngwevu's senior apprentices stood up and said that we had all been blessed by the ancestors, and "*Siyabulela kakhulu.*" (We give heartfelt thanks.) Tat' uSukwini stood up again and said, "*Izinyanya ziyavuma!*" (The ancestors have agreed!) The ancestors had accepted all our prayers, and it was clear that they approved my final sangoma initiation ceremony: umgoduso.

The spiritual experiences we had witnessed that morning were now feeding the community. The story of our morning ritual was being told, every word solidifying our connection to the sea and forest people. As the elders spoke, the young children listened and passed what they had heard to other children, who ran down the road to carry these words farther afield. The message was clear: "The people of the waters had spoken." Passersby on the road paused and heard the elders and then continued their journeys with a lighter step and more spiritual confidence. Their walk said, "The old ways are alive. The ancestors have spoken."

## TRADITIONAL SACRIFICE (BLOOD MIXED WITH SPIRIT)

At around 3 p.m. my goat ceremony began. We started in the house, with Tata acting the part of the elder master of ceremonies, or chief (induna, or *inkosi*). He told everyone we would announce to the ancestors the beginning of my umgoduso ceremony through the sacrifice of the goat, whose blood would open the way for my final ceremony. It was considered good manners, and a vital part of showing respect to the ancestors, to sacrifice a goat before an ox. The goat would act as an emissary from the world of the living, greeting the ancestors over the waters and telling them we intended to sacrifice an ox in a few days to complete my sangoma training.

As we sacrifice the goat, part of its spirit connects to the person for whom it is being sacrificed. The initiate sangoma thus becomes more intuitive and connected to the natural world, and the intuitive wisdom we receive can then benefit all life. After a goat sacrifice, the sangoma is given the goat's skin to use for ancestral prayers, a sign of our commitment to connect to the ancestors and the Great Spirit, the omniscient spirit of nature.

We gathered in the kraal to witness the sacrifice. The elders asked the ancestors to accept the offering of the goat to open the way for Roman. All the elders and sangomas were given an opportunity to call in their ancestors and honor their people. When it was my turn, I thanked the goat for the sacrifice it was about to make. I asked it to greet all my ancestors on the other side and bring them to my final initiation ceremony in a few days' time. I placed my hand on the goat's body, allowing the heat from my hands to move from my heart into the goat, as a form of silent prayer. I was sad, but knew in my heart that we were following an ancient road with signposts written in the land and nature.

The goat was treated with dignity. Two men held it while Tata covered its body with the white foam of *isilawu*, a medicinal plant we use for all our initiation ceremonies to connect to our ancestors and the spirit realm. The goat was offered some isilawu to drink, and as it drank, the community chanted "Camagu!" Then the goat was placed on its side. Tata slit the goat's throat efficiently and quickly. As it died, it cried out, "Aaaaaaaa!" The people screamed as one, "Camagu!" as the goat flew like a lightning bird into the other world. The people were happy because they saw the goat's cry as a good omen and a clear sign that the ancestors and nature spirits had accepted our sacrifice. We were in alignment with them, and the community responded with an encore of jubilation and relief.

My body shook, as if electrified, and a part of me was traveling over the waters to the world of my ancestors. I felt the vortex energy of my dreams being fed by the goat's blood, which was like rain after a lengthy drought—our spirits were being watered and nourished. The community started singing and dancing. The drums rolled, and the ground beneath my feet moved to the earthy rhythms and hypnotic isiXhosa clicks that seemed to melt into Mother Earth.

I was guided to a reed mat a few feet from my goat. A blanket was wrapped around me and I was encouraged to sit quietly. Few words were said to me, but I understood what was happening: I was to absorb the goat's spirit and follow it to the other world. Part of me felt very tired, while another part was waking up. I was in the liminal world now, traveling quickly through the world of my ancestors.

The kraal was a buzz of energy, with men running to and fro organizing the space. A few dry slivers of wood were placed on the ground near the goat's oozing body. A match was struck with a steady hand and gently offered to the dry wood, which sucked on it eagerly. Long tendrils of smoke reached for the heavens. The first smoke was seen as a blessing as the people allowed the smoke to move through and around them, as if they too were being touched by the spirit world. The crackling fire was mirrored by the giggles and clicks of the people. I felt a deep sense of harmony and balance around me—the earth was alive beneath my reed mat.

The goat's body was dismembered with grace and skill. The innards were taken out and cooked in pots on the fire, and the skin was gently peeled off and placed discreetly nearby. With open hearts and faces, the elders offered me the first meat from my goat, an opportunity to deepen my connection with the goat and the sacrifice it had made. The meat was sweet and tasty. The elders were happy. The umsebenzi was deemed a success.

To receive something magical and sublime often requires great sacrifice. The sangoma world is inextricably linked to the cycle of life and death, for we are nature/spirit doctors. And this teaching is the hardest to absorb because of our attachment to life. For me to be reborn spiritually, something had to die. The goat had died, but part of it now lived inside of me. I was becoming a complete sangoma.

I sat on my mat for hours. Township life moved around me. I became incandescent as I wavered like a candle between the worlds. Then I was pulled out of my reverie by children relaying messages to me from MaMngwevu. My sangoma colleagues came to collect me as the first drops of rain fell. The sky had darkened and thunder clouds loomed. I heard, "*Imvula vintsikelelo! Izinyanya ziyavuya ngoku!*" (The rain is a blessing! The ancestors are very happy now!) The sun set over the horizon while the elder men debated and the community moved to the rhythm of a forgotten time.

Men and women, old and young, gathered in and outside the kraal space. Everyone was being fed the goat meat and umqombothi. In turn, we all drank from the same pail and ate from the same pots, thus strengthening our innate Ubuntu. The presence of large numbers of people was seen as a blessing because they brought their songs and ancestors with them.

Nothing was wasted. I saw some of the poorest people in the township arrive, stick thin and in threadbare clothes. Their faces spoke of despair, and the ceremony filled them both physically and spiritually. They left hours later with a lightness in their being. They too were replenished by the goat, and I felt proud to have hosted this remarkable event.

A few days later the final stage of my initiation began, merging with Roman. A makeshift canvas hut was built inside the kraal. I was encouraged to rest inside it while I sat on a reed mat under a blanket. The purpose of the hut was to be close to Roman, to absorb his spirit and become one with him.

Now Roman was just a few yards away from me. I felt comfortable in his wild presence as he stomped around the kraal space. I could hear him breathing. I felt an electrical pulse building, like the atmosphere before a thunderstorm. I heard the steady beat of the drums. New sangomas were arriving, greeted by the others in song. After a few minutes the songs changed—the clicks and melodies were different from anything I had heard before. I felt dizzy and sleepy, but I couldn't sleep; my body was charged with electricity. I felt a pulse moving up and down my body. Roman was getting more agitated, and his breathing became more pronounced. I shouted out to him, but my voice didn't belong to me: "*Roman, xola mtshanam, xola!*" (Roman, calm down, my friend, calm down!)

Roman started pounding his feet in time to the drums and banging his head against the nearby hedge. He bellowed a few times, shaking the walls. Cows in the neighborhood responded. The night was waking up. The sangomas and their apprentices sang and danced through the night. Every fiber and cell in my body danced and moved to the trance-inducing tunes. Even the animals—dogs, goats, donkeys, and cattle—seemed to sway like waves. In their eyes I saw a twinkle of encouragement and a hint of excitement. The sounds were evocative and sweet. I loved the voices as they climbed higher and shattered the air with their clicks like a crackling fire. There was an ebb and flow to the rhythms mirroring the tides of the sea. Life and death became one long wave of highs and lows, with a shaking in the middle.

## OX SACRIFICE—THE FINAL INITIATION

My final day of initiation began with the dawn chorus: baying donkeys and bellowing cows led by Roman. Again, I was led into the makeshift hut in the kraal near my ox. I was encouraged to sit quietly and absorb his primeval wildness; my spirit was encouraged to merge with his. My thoughts wandered briefly to my Zen training and the Zen ox herding pictures that reflect the stages of enlightenment. In these pictures the ox represents the shadowy, fragmented parts of our soul that we need to befriend.[2] Our task is to befriend them with patience, kindness, and discipline, just like Tat' uSukwini's taming of Roman.

The final ox herding picture shows the man riding the ox, representing a merging of the shadow: ego, heart, and mind. I was experiencing this. I had been practicing Zen meditation for more than fifteen years, and now all the stages of the ox herding pictures were moving through me—a call to merge with the wildness within me, my raw primeval, instinctual connection to nature. It was a call to connect my heart with my mind. And deeper still, it represented a marriage of me to my izinyanya. The shamans of old all went through serious rites of passage to signify a marriage to their guardian or nature spirits. They were dream walkers, inhabiting two worlds—the world of the living and the world of spirit. I was about to engage with this ancient ritual, and I was afraid.

Now there were hundreds of people present from all over the Eastern Cape. I was the first white person in recent history to finish the Xhosa sangoma training. The people of Tat' uSukwini's clan had come to check me out and see what all the fuss was about. It was also an opportunity for old friends to meet—a traditional festival. My parents and old friends were there, a few white faces in a sea of brown, like vanilla flakes on chocolate ice cream. The sun beat down, and it was about one hundred degrees in the shade. We all melted together, creating an exciting new taste. I was hot beneath my blanket in the hut, but at least I was in the shade. The songs and drumming shook the earth beneath me, like a low-grade earthquake. All the elders started to gather in the kraal, supported by the senior sangomas, resplendent in their beads and colorful turbans.

It was an auspicious day for my father's family: the day of my grandfather's passing, January 20. We had figured this would be the best day to celebrate my coming of age as a senior sangoma. Tat' uSukwini opened the kraal space by blessing the entrance, the back of the kraal, and the totem pole in the center with brandy. Roman was tied to the totem pole. He bellowed, shaking our nerves and enlivening our senses. Tata asked his ancestors and the Great Spirit to accept the sacrifice of Roman as an offering for my umgoduso. Tata spoke about my arrival at his home ten years earlier, and said that I had become his adopted son. He spoke about my gift of dreams and how I had dreamed each stage of my igqirha training in the ways of the Xhosa people.

MaMngwevu followed Tat' uSukwini, calling on all her ancestors to support us and bless me. She spoke about my gifts and praised me for being humble. She said I was very respectful of her and her husband and had quickly become a part of her family. She commended my parents for bringing me up in such a good way. She spoke about the difficulty involved in becoming a full sangoma and how we are all tested, and that it is important for us to be humble, to pray to our ancestors and uThixo, and to listen to our dreams. When times are tough we need to endure and trust in God and our ancestors. MaMngwevu spoke about her own training under MaNwabe, her teacher, and some of the lessons she learned. Today was a good day, and she was delighted to see that I was finishing after all these years of training.

I was sitting on the ground on my reed mat, a few meters from the totem pole. After MaMngwevu and Tat' uSukwini finished speaking, I was asked to say a few words or do a *nqula* (ancestor-praising) prayer. I stood and said my name and honored my ancestors and the Great Spirit. I called on all my ancestors to please accept Roman as my offering. I thanked my ancestors and God for bringing me to the Sukwini home and training me in this ancient way. I also thanked my parents and MaMngwevu and Tat' uSukwini for their grace and hospitality. I finished by thanking Roman for coming to me in my dreams and for the sacrifice he was about to make. I sat down again.

Other sangomas stood up to speak. The kraal hummed to an atmosphere of dignity and decorum. Then the drums played and the sangomas chanted and danced, lifting a veil of dust into the air amid the sounds of children laughing, dogs barking, and the occasional bellow of donkeys in the distance.

Tata moved like a ballet dancer in the kraal. He took off his shoes and offered instructions to the men to hold Roman. They held the ox with ropes and encouraged him to lie down, treating him with great respect and a firm but gentle hand. He bellowed, and the sangomas chanted, "Camagu!" The drums continued, the dust lifted higher, and the sun beat down upon us, burning away everything that was untrue and insincere. Tata moved around Roman, blessing his entire body with the white isilawu that would help connect Roman with our ancestors. Roman bellowed, sending up a chorus of answering bellows from cows in the vicinity.

Then Tata offered Roman some isilawu to drink. He wet his lips on the white foam. Tata placed the isilawu pail on the ground behind him. Then, with one movement, he plunged his knife into Roman's neck, at the base of his skull. Roman sent out an earth-shattering bellow, and the sangomas chanted, "Camagu!" Roman bellowed and the sangomas chanted while Tata moved the knife toward Roman's throat, slicing it completely and opening a river of blood into the nearby buckets and the ground beneath our feet.

A shudder of electricity went through me as Roman bellowed and died. His spirit moved like lightning toward the spirit world. I felt dizzy and lightheaded as part of me joined Roman in his journey to the ancestors. I briefly caught Tata's eye. He held my gaze and said gently to me, "*Cingo, uhambe kakuhle!*" (John, he went well!)" Roman had gone quickly into the other world without too much pain. I could sense Tata's steely determination—this wasn't easy for either of us, but we were committed to connecting with our ancestors in this ancient tradition.

All the sangomas stood up at once, dancing and singing the community into the world of the ancestors. Three large drums were played, with new drummers stepping in as others tired. There was such a sense of celebration and relief! The women ululated, "*Halala, halala, halala!*" (It is done!) I had completed my final step in becoming an igqirha.

I sat on my reed mat, feeling like I was standing at the threshold of two worlds, the living and the dead. But the dead were alive with spirit, and Roman's blood created a portal of life rushing from our world into the dreamtime. My dreams converged into a single place, and I was fully in the present moment. My reed mat was like a magic carpet surrounded by light. The ground beneath me no longer felt so solid—I sensed life everywhere. Roman's blood was creating more life and connection around me. I was in a magical African portal where life converged, changed, and moved.

Men began running around the kraal area, chopping wood, lighting a fire, and dismembering Roman's carcass bone by bone. I watched Roman's body change shape, being cut into pieces quietly and efficiently, as I watched his spirit slip into the dreamtime. Life and death felt like one cycle, with death another form of life: the spiritual life. Roman's body was cooked in large pots and parts of him were later distributed to the community. Again, I was offered the first meat, followed by the elders and other sangomas. Everyone was offered a piece of Roman, and he carried on living inside the bodies of hundreds of people.

I felt shattered and overwhelmed. I sat meditating on my reed mat for hours, watching Roman's body disintegrate in front of me. His beautiful red coat was rolled up and stored away to be preserved so I could hold his memory close to my heart. His skull and horns were put in a special place.

People were happily eating, drinking, and enjoying one another's company. I was happy about this, as I knew the hard life that many of them endured in the township. Meat was a luxury, and for many people, especially the elderly and young, this ceremony was an opportunity to feast and replenish their bodies and souls.

As the sun set, I heard the sound of thunder rolling over the nearby hills. Some of Mama's grandchildren came running toward me with eager smiles. They said, "*Umama uyakubiza, hamba ngena Phakathi!*" (Mother is calling you. You can go inside now!) I went to the back of the house to rest. People called out to me as I left, offering encouragement, gratitude, and thanks. I felt so humbled to be appreciated by the local township people—my heart was bursting with gratitude. When I reached the back room, I collapsed in a heap. People brought me food and drink. I was suddenly very hungry.

That night the sangomas danced. We danced for our ancestors. We danced for uThixo. We danced for one another, our community, and Roman. We danced to demonstrate our gratitude for such a wonderful ceremony. We danced our pain and suffering and allowed our spines and spirits to welcome in umoya.

I welcomed the new spirit of Roman inside of me and danced my new spiritual energy and strength. We thanked the Great Spirit for everything we had experienced together. As we danced, we recommitted ourselves to our sangoma calling. Our words were filled with gratitude and appreciation. The walls moved to the sounds of the drum, and the little house heaved under the pressure of all the people. As we danced, we became spiritual warriors from a forgotten time. We each had our sticks, which we used to whip our bodies into higher states of ecstasy. Our voices boomed across the valley of death to the world of our ancestors. We beseeched them, pleaded with them, and loved them. As we roared the names of forefathers and mothers, we remembered who we were and our life path was clear in front of us.

We danced to raise the energy of the home and community, to push the shadow of discontent and hopelessness away. Even if we could do it for only one night, we would achieve success, creating a moment of timelessness where everything slowed down, where the rhythms were intoxicating and people could connect with the vortex of life, the source of all things. Then they could connect with their ancestors and receive meaningful dreams for their lives. The room spun faster and faster. I saw myself as a black man. I merged with the group. We danced so quickly and dynamically that a portal or vortex energy was created and I slipped into the dreamtime of my ancestors.

The next day I woke to the sound of braying donkeys, barking dogs, and the cheerful laughter of my sangoma colleagues in the nearby room. My body felt tired but my spirit felt relieved. I heard people talking about dreams. I got up and said good morning to my friends and family members. I was excited to hear that people in the home had received good dreams; this was a sign that we sangomas had succeeded in helping our community connect with the ancient ones. I noticed Tat' uSukwini, who winked at me, and I joined him outside. We spoke about the ceremony while he pulled on his cigarette and we watched the township come to life.

Tata said, "*Cingo, umsembenzi mhle, umoya uphezulu!*" (Cingo, the ceremony was beautiful, the spiritual energy was lifted up.)

"*Ewe, Tat' am, enkosi kakhulu!*" (Yes, my father, thank you so much!) I replied.

We gathered in the kraal one more time. I sat on my reed mat. All the sangomas and elders wore their finest clothes. I marveled at their colorful beads, dignity, and stately presence. I watched as all the senior sangomas gathered in the kraal, their apprentices waiting outside, stretched over drums with pensive, expectant expressions on their faces.

Tat' uSukwini opened the kraal space in his customary fashion, calling on his ancestors and honoring them and the Great Spirit. He proclaimed the ceremony a success and mentioned the signs and how Roman had bellowed, indicating that the ancestors had accepted our sacrifice. Local people peeked through the hedge and reached cameras above their heads to take pictures of me. I felt like a celebrity.

The fire was still burning as Roman's body was being offered to the local community, and his blood continued to connect all of us. I listened to the elders' speeches. MaMngwevu praised her ancestors and the Great Spirit. She also praised my family and thanked my parents for traveling to join us. She spoke about the pain of my calling and what I had gone through. She talked about her dream the night before I arrived of uThixo telling her to be ready to train someone from another culture. Tears flowed down her face as she described how sick I was with the thwasa, how skinny I was, and how I struggled to find a way to get better. She said she had no idea how she was going to teach me because we did not speak one another's language, but that she trusted in uThixo. She thanked me for coming to her home and being so gracious. She also thanked uThixo for giving her this experience because she learned a great deal. And she said she was extremely happy today to be putting my new beads on me, completing my journey home from the ancestral world and signifying the end of my sangoma apprenticeship.

I stood and thanked everyone for attending my ceremony and giving me such love and support. I praised my ancestors and the Great

Tat' uSukwini, John, and MaMngwevu
after John's final initiation ceremony.
PHOTO COURTESY OF KANINA FOSS, 2007

Spirit uThixo and asked that they bless the people and help them always remember their ancestors. I also asked the ancient ones to help the people move out of poverty so they could lead happier, more fulfilled lives. When I finished speaking everyone responded, "Camagu!"

Then my elders encouraged my dad to speak, which took him by surprise. His voice breaking with emotion, he simply thanked everyone for showing such love and support for his son. The wind dropped, and the air was very quiet.

My dad is six feet four. He towered above a sea of black faces in the heart of one of the poorest black African communities in South Africa. They had never seen a white man of my father's generation speaking with such emotion and humility in their midst. I could feel the emotions stirring around me. Some of the ladies had tears in their eyes, as my father's words struck a deep chord inside them. The words were another confirmation of the end of apartheid; now South Africans, no matter their socioeconomic or cultural backgrounds, had the opportunity to help one another. As he finished talking, there was a loud round of applause and I saw many teary faces. I felt a part of the historical shift in South Africa.

All the senior sangomas stood up to honor their ancestors and offer me a teaching and blessing. As each sangoma finished speaking, the community responded with "Camagu!" Drums rolled, feet stomped, dust rose, and children laughed happily. The sun beat down ferociously on me, burning away my past as the ceremony opened the door to my future.

Tat' uSukwini approached me with Roman's tail attached to a staff of wood. He presented the oxtail, called an *itshoba*, to me. He asked me to put my hands out with palms facing up. He placed the itshoba on my hands three times; the third time he left it there. He placed isilawu foam on the itshoba and covered my hands with it. He encouraged the nearby sangomas to also place isilawu foam on my eyes, ears, and crown. I was instructed to drink the white foam; it had a strong, woody herb taste.

Then the sangomas brought me new beads. They first blessed them with isilawu foam and then gently placed the beads upon me until my entire body was dressed in shiny new colorful beads: a crown of beads was placed around my forehead, and beads were wrapped around my neck, wrists, elbows, and ankles. I was adorned like a king. New white garments were equally blessed and wrapped around my body, and a colorful turban was wrapped around my head. To finish my dress, white clay was discreetly pasted around my eyes.

I stood tall, like a prince in the Sukwini, Ngwevu, Kelly, and Lockley families, with one ceremonial stick in each hand, staring into the fire of Roman's transformation. My gaze drawn up toward the horizon, I watched as the tail of Comet McNaught spread across the sky. This was a very auspicious sign as it raced across the skies for the full seven days of my initiation. I was thirty-five years old, and my old life was now over. The people ululated, "Halala, halala!" finishing with "Camagu! Camagu! Camagu! Camagu!"

At last, I had completed my sangoma apprenticeship, and the people celebrated my return to the world.

# 13

# Entering the Shadowlands

After my initiation I was completely exhausted and spent the next three weeks in bed. I sweated through my nightly journeys, waking hot, as if burned by the volcanic intensity of the source of life itself. It felt like my cellular system was being rewired, my DNA changed. I didn't remember my dreams—very unusual for me. MaMngwevu told me I was just tired and my spirits were giving me a rest.

I moved into the dreamtime world to regain my strength. Once, I caught an image of a leopard in the periphery of my vision. He seemed to sway and dance, inviting me into the shadowlands of my spirit between dreaming and wakefulness, into my inner landscape. There was a hint of danger about him, as if he was silently warning me to be careful.

Lifting the veil between ignorance and wisdom comes at a price. I had felt that price, experiencing all manner of human deceit and betrayal, seeing the ugly side of existence and humanity's sadness. Yet the joy of an African sunset, the innocence of animals' eyes, and the beauty of a baby's laughter inspired me to delve deeper into the shadowlands. Sangomas live in the liminal spaces between shadow and light, for therein lies the truth.

I kept hearing the words of Zen Master Su Bong: "Go beyond good and bad, light and dark, and I will meet you in that place." The human world is full of right and wrong. In this, nature is the master teacher. The oak tree never looks at the lavender bush with arrogance and deceit. And when the sun shines, it blesses both good and bad without distinction. Tracking nature lets us see life with an innocent eye and an openness of heart and mind. Ancient mystics knew this and used the natural world to steer people to a place of harmony and balance. A friend of mine, Craig Foster, who worked alongside Bushmen trackers in the Kalahari Desert, once said that connecting with nature is like connecting with the living face of God.

Comet McNaught, also known as the Great Comet of 2007, was said to be the brightest in decades.[1] Tracking it through the night sky awoke old memories and signified for me the culmination of my sangoma calling, and as its tail stretched into the northern sky, it evoked thoughts about my future work. I was at a loss about what to do with the rest of my life. All my energies had been dedicated to training and learning. I listened to my dreams and spirits to show me my new road.

One night a friend of mine who had witnessed my graduation ceremony pointed to the comet and said, "That mirrors you, John. Now you will take the magic of the sangoma to the Northern Hemisphere." I smiled nonchalantly, feeling spent and exhausted from all the ceremonies, prayers, and dreams. I felt like a soldier after a long war. Most warfare starts with people's inner pain and wounds, which they project onto the world outside. I was no different. In order to become a "wounded healer," I had to make peace with my own pain and vulnerability. I had pieced together fragmented and alienated parts of myself. I had heard the call of my ancestors and brought them into me. Now my work was becoming clear: to help people find their own way home to themselves and their ancestors.

My body, mind, and spirit were absorbing the magnitude of my initiation; I waited for a sign from the dreamtime to show me a reflection of it. Fortunately, it wasn't long before I experienced a profound dream that clarified my new spirit.

I was back at high school after my graduation ceremony, walking the long corridors. Then I was walking along the playing fields outside. A kraal appeared in one of the fields. In its center appeared a tall totem pole displaying the faces of my animal spirits. An eagle circled above me, its face changing to that of a sphinx. I looked at the images but listened to the deeper knowing within my body and bones. Then a bolt of electricity ran down the totem pole, energizing my spirit and waking me up in a visceral, elemental way.

The next day, while I meditated on the night sky, I noticed the comet's tail turning into the tail of the leopard, who called me to remember my blood people, the European nations inside of me who were at war with themselves because they had forgotten who they were. I felt called to the Northern Hemisphere to help my blood people connect to their ancestors. I was about to embark on a seven-year pilgrimage that would take me around the world and to the European nations of my forebears.

My graduation dream helped me connect with a deeper ancestral memory inside of me. My father had given me the ring of my great-grandfather, who came from England as a merchant marine in the early 1900s and jumped ship in Durban. The ring held the Lockley family emblem, a griffin with a key in its mouth. Like many English surnames, our name reflected our earlier vocations: we were locksmiths. I had always been mesmerized by the magical power of doors to unlock both physical and spiritual roads. Now my ancestral name was being reforged in Africa. I was now a spiritual locksmith. My job was simple: to help people unlock the doors to their inner homes and connect to their ancestral birthright, releasing their gifts and spiritual calling in this world. Everyone is called, and when people answer the call of their spirit, true happiness is achieved and balance and harmony are created in their communities, hence strengthening Ubuntu.

As the months after my initiation turned into years, I noticed my body changing. I seemed to fill out, and my feet even grew one size—amazing at the age of thirty-five. For the first time in my life I actually started to put on weight. This was a clear sign that my thwasa illness had improved and my new life was beginning.

# 14

# Initiation as Transformation

## TRANSFORMING CHAOS ENERGY

A key ingredient in all initiations is heightened emotions. As water starts to boil, steam is emitted. During times of communal initiations such as weddings or baptisms, I encourage people to watch their emotional bodies but not react to them. Life is imbued with opposites, the most literal being death. The opposite energy to initiation is chaos, or discordant energy, which helps fuel the energy of initiation. The challenge is always to focus on the burning wood and not the smoke of the emotions.

Some of the most powerful forces in nature are swirling storms—tornados and hurricanes. They are a wonderful metaphor for spiritual transformation. We evolve in a spiral fashion, sometimes returning to old patterns of behavior that don't serve us in order for us to break through and create new ways of functioning in the world.

With each new twist in the spiral, our consciousness expands, impacting our cells, bones, DNA, and spirit; and this in turn impacts the next generation, our unborn children. As with childbirth, the sweetness of new life comes at a warrior's price: pain and suffering. If we become attached to our pain, we miss the point. Transformation has to be difficult—otherwise it wouldn't mean anything.

The spiral of transformation contains umbilini energy, the bittersweet elixir of spiraling electrical mystery that moves up and down the spine. This spiral moves laterally as well as vertically, breaking down the barriers between ourselves and the rest of the world. A great deal has been written about kundalini energy from the yogic perspective in India. For us in Africa, the electrical heat of the umbilini energy, or umoya, is ignited through initiation, prayers, and dancing. I experienced it as a supreme intelligence gently encouraging me to move beyond the confines of my narrow worldview and think of the world as an extension of myself. After my initiation, my thoughts and actions were imbued with a new energy and power, with the potential to affect both the dreamtime and living world.

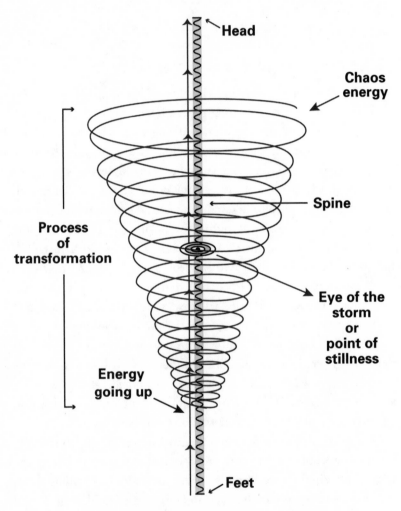

Vertical spiral demonstrating the movement
and transformation of chaos energy.

## INITIATION AS A BLESSING CEREMONY

Initiation in the Xhosa culture involves an intricate blessing ceremony in which the elders transmit the teachings and wisdom of the
tribe to the initiate to help the initiate develop as a healer or an elder
in the community, and help the world. The initiation culminates
with the head medicine person—in my case, my sangoma teacher—
anointing the initiate using herbs, beads, and prayers.

Our DNA and cellular memories hold ancient wisdom that can
be passed on by word of mouth, activating seeds of wisdom from
one generation to the next. This is why spiritual lineages are very
important. When people have a calling to study shamanism, I always
recommend that they study from someone who is connected with a
living shamanic lineage going back in time. A teacher is merely a vessel

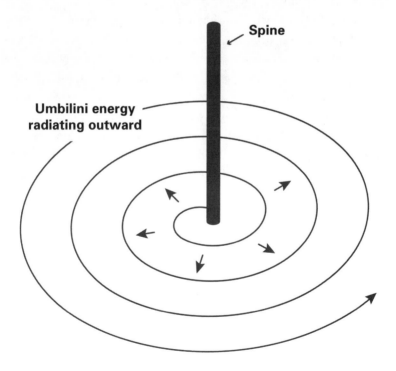

Lateral spiral demonstrating the movement of umbilini energy.

or channel of mystical teachings connecting us with our beginning, the dreamtime. When we are connected to an ancient stream, there is less of an attachment to the selfish ego.

There are many mystical lineages with roots stretching back thousands of years. In Korean Zen, for instance, a Zen master initiates a student into mastery through a process called "transmission": transmitting the "dharma teachings" from master to student energetically, from mind to mind. This can only happen when the student is ready, and the master decides this. The seal of approval for this initiation is a specially carved Zen stick. In the sangoma apprenticeship, it is the tail of the ox, ornately beaded and placed on the end of a stick. Ancient traditions put great faith in the sacred umbilini or kundalini energy to open our hearts and minds and connect us to the world around us. As we are rooted in the earth via direct experience, it makes sense that we are then rewarded with a simple stick.

I have told you much about the initiation ceremonies I undertook to become a sangoma. Due to the sacred nature of this ancient tradition, I am duty bound not to reveal them all. But I can say that after each initiation ceremony, I recognized the pattern of transformation and how my life changed.

First came the sangoma dream. It always arrived with a lot of energy, like touching a bolt of lightning or being caught up in a hurricane. Then I discussed the dream with my elders, going down on my knees and burning sacred impepho, honoring my ancestors, uThixo, and my teachers, and then recounting my dream. My elders sat still and listened, while outside a storm started brewing. It could be a literal storm—rain clouds rolling over the countryside—or come in the form of animals and children getting a burst of energy. Goats might come knocking on the divination room door followed by children demanding their grandmother's attention for sweets or something else.

After many years of initiations and dreams, I started to recognize a particular pattern emerging: as soon as my dream left my body, it seemed to take on a life of its own in the outer world, affecting the weather and life outside the shrine house. I called it chaos energy because it had a vital quality, like a living being. Each sangoma initiation ceremony carried its own distinctive quality, opening my body and intuition and drawing me closer to the natural world and my beloved township community. Once I had recounted my dream, I kept quiet. My elders paused, thought, and breathed, and then MaMngwevu spoke. As the leader of our medicine lineage, it was important for her to confirm that I had indeed experienced a sangoma initiation dream, which then required an initiation ceremony. Once the date was confirmed, I noticed a new intensity in my life. I had made a decision, as witnessed by my elders, to go deeper into my calling, into my spirit. I would climb higher and in so doing let the ancestors burn away any chaff that might hinder my spiritual evolvement. The umbilini energy in my spine was reactivated—as if responding to an electrical current turned on full, my hands shook and my body vibrated. My elders smiled. After our interview, Mama gave me more herbs to drink and wash in. There is nothing like the green of nature to calm the nerves and appease the renewed energy in the spine.

I experienced this transformational energy as a storm. My emotions were heightened, as were my feelings, intuitions, and dreams. One of the strongest teachings I learned was not to react to my emotions, as they built like a tornado right up to the ceremony. During these times of heightened turmoil, I needed to feel my spine and the bones in my body, which helped balance and ground me. The eye in the hurricane of my transformation was my spine and the breath inside my spine. At night I closed my eyes and felt the shaking in my body. My heart raced like a wild horse. As I noticed it and breathed through my spine and into the ground, the electrical impulse inside of me calmed down.

The mark of transformational experiences such as initiation is the effect it has on our nervous system. All lives are full of transformational moments where our spirits are called to climb higher and reach deeper inside ourselves. One of the indications of a transformational or initiatory experience is the degree of chaos around us and nervous tension inside. A wedding, Holy Communion, and baptism are some examples of transformational or initiatory experiences in the modern world. Yet these are also ancient ceremonies that test our nerves, emotions, and commitment.

When we feel this upheaval, the best course is to feel our bones, listen to our heartbeat, and center ourselves. This is how we feel at one with life and find our way toward peace.

# PART VI

Out of Africa

# 15

# A Seven-Year Pilgrimage

## One Truth, Many Cultures

The divining winds of Africa pointed me toward distant shores, and over a number of years I became like a swallow, living a perpetual summer by chasing the warm weather from the Southern to the Northern Hemisphere and back again.

As I traveled, I discovered that no matter where we live, when we honor our ancestors, we khanya (shine). The reason for this is simple. Honoring the blood in our veins and the gift of life activates an old alchemical system of transformation in the human soul. We start to dream about our ancestors, and they show us how we can remember who we are and the people we come from. They help us discover our gifts and calling in the world. This was my experience worldwide as I left South Africa and visited the United Kingdom, Ireland, Belgium, France, Germany, Holland, Denmark, Japan, the United States, Mexico, and Canada.

I led many workshops and retreats and learned the songs and ways of the people I worked with. People often told me they had dreamed about a leopard before I arrived. I taught them about Ubuntu and how to use their blood and bones as a living electrical circuit to connect with their ancestors and come home to themselves. They in turn taught me about their own cultures. These trips were blessed; numerous people dreamed about their ancestors after my ceremonies, and I reconnected to missing ancestral pieces within my soul.

The landscape of our dreams reflects our ancestry. For years in South Africa, I dreamed about a seascape that looked different from the sea I was familiar with. Later, when I lived on the west coast of Ireland a few hours from my Kelly family's roots, these dream images made sense. The land on which our ancestors walk leaves an indelible impression on our DNA. For those who want to connect with their people, I always recommend walking the land of their ancestors. The smell and the tactical sense of the land initiate a cycle of remembering. The hair at the base of your spine can tingle when you experience something profound, mysterious, and ancient. The land of your forebears will have this effect on you.

## AN AFRO-CELT HEALER RETURNS TO IRELAND

I returned to Ireland as a sangoma, an ancestrally initiated Afro-Celt shaman, having completed my initiation by marrying my ancestors to my spirit. I was looking forward to what awaited me in my maternal homeland.

My pilgrimage started in Galway, my old Irish home. I was invited to a book launch in Waterford City, and there the healing energy that had been transmitted into me kicked into high gear. A friend asked me to perform my traditional Xhosa trance dance. I was accompanied by a well-known musician who played my isigubu (sangoma drum) and managed to pick up the particular sangoma rhythm enough for me to go into trance. My energy soared like an eagle, and I called on my ancestors in isiXhosa to bless my friends. It was a strong experience for me, and the building shook to my stomping feet.

Afterward, a lady named Sharon approached me and shared a painful story about her daughter's boyfriend, Conor, who had dived into a swimming pool in Donegal and broken his neck. He was rushed to the Mater Hospital in Dublin and was currently in the intensive care unit.

A few days later, Sharon phoned me. She told me she had been struck by the energy that came off me when I danced and wondered if I could do anything to help Conor. I felt transported back to 1991 and 1 Military Hospital in Pretoria, when I prayed to be shown a healing technique I could use if ever I was called on to help someone as critically ill as my patient Emmanuel. Now I was a sangoma, and I was being asked to work in an intensive care unit again.

I asked if Conor was mentally alert, and if so to please ask him if he would like me to work with him. MaMngwevu had once visited my parents and told them I had a healing gift in my hands. This gift had now matured, and Conor's illness was an opportunity for me to do my work. I was excited, but I didn't want to give the family false hope because I had no idea whether I could help Conor or not. I said the best I could probably do was to help him with the trauma he was experiencing. In reply, they asked me to come to Dublin as soon as I could.

I prayed by the sea near Galway. I collected some stones, seaweed, and water from the nearby rock pools. I called on my ancestral spirits, the spirits of the sea, and my nature spirits from Africa to give me the energy I needed to assist with Conor's healing. I looked for signs from the sea. I heard the cry of a seagull close by and saw a stirring in the kelp fields.

At the hospital, I was quickly ushered to Conor's bedside in the ICU. He was lying awash in medical machines, his face alert. Apparently, he felt nothing from his neck down. He greeted me with a friendly smile and thanked me for taking the time to come to his aid. I was impressed with his stoic, uncomplaining attitude, reminiscent of the soldiers I had looked after so long ago. Evidently, Conor had nearly died. Sometimes those who have almost crossed over have a new lease on life. I felt this in his presence.

I told Conor that I would apply round stones to pressure points on his body and use my hands to heat the stones. I needed Conor to work with me, so I led him on a guided meditation. Fortunately, he could control his breathing, so I encouraged him to breathe all the way down into his belly—long, slow, mindful breaths. He closed his eyes.

I said a silent prayer to my spirits, asking them to come into me. Then I chanted in isiXhosa. I closed my eyes and saw a ray of light coming into me—I directed it toward Conor. I felt the exquisite energy of the trance dance enter me like a gurgling stream with a delightful golden glow.

My body suddenly went through a number of changes. My heartbeat increased dramatically, and I could feel it all the way to my fingertips. My body temperature increased, and my hands became incredibly hot. I moved quickly, soaking the round pebbles with seawater and kelp and then applying one stone at a time to Conor's body. I placed a large stone on his center, below his belly button. I held my hand on the stone with a gentle pressure to stimulate the energy meridian in this part of his body. A fiery heat went through my hands and into the stone. After a few minutes, I noticed Conor's stomach becoming warmer. I placed stones on the soles of his feet. I then went to his hands and finished with my hands gently touching his head, allowing the heat to move through me. Conor became very tired, and after an hour's work it was time to leave him.

As I walked down the corridors of the hospital, I felt like an electrical rod of energy. I was very thirsty and needed to drink lots of water. Conor's mother thanked me for the treatment, and when I shook her hand she was amazed by the heat in mine.

I felt the completion of a cycle that began in 1990 with Emmanuel's mother asking me if he was going to live or not. Now in 2007, Conor's mother was nervously asking me if I thought her son would walk again. I was struck by the similarities between the two cases, but now I didn't feel so paralyzed about how to help. My training and apprenticeship had paid off. I was able to step in where modern medicine had reached a crossroads. I had realized my calling and became an igqirha, the one who holds the lightning rod of the ancestors.

A few hours after I left, Conor's body went into a healing fever. When it broke, he was surprisingly better in many ways and more alert. His medical staff moved him out of the ICU into a ward dealing with spinal injuries.

I worked with him twice more, and both times the heat went flooding through my body. On my third treatment I noticed a change in Conor's body. I asked him to close his eyes and tell me if he could feel anything. I applied pressure to the sole of his right foot and then pulled my hand away. He said, "Yes. I feel a tingle under my right foot." His mother burst into tears.

Conor's body got stronger and stronger. When I visited him again about three weeks later, he had been moved to a rehabilitation center. I saw him moving across the grounds, assisted by a man on his right. Conor wore a big smile on his face—he was walking!

I'm not exactly sure what I did to help Conor. Maybe with modern medicine he would have walked again anyway, but I think I helped him release the trauma his body held. Trauma is an emotional and physical response to a sudden shock to the body. The heat from my body, added to the acupressure points on his, helped relax him and release his trauma.

Every human being has the ability to use heat to heal because we are elemental creatures of the earth. Just as birds navigate wind currents with their wings and feathers, we have the ability to navigate our breath and direct heat to different parts of our bodies. All it takes is patience, mindfulness, and the intention to help another being. I have used this technique on animals and plants with surprising effectiveness. All life works according to the principles of heat. When the life force flickers as a result of trauma and we apply heat with our hands and heart, something changes. New life blossoms.

My sangoma training taught me how to connect to the primal, visceral, and elemental side of my humanity. It taught me how to use my body to heal. It also taught me how to pray in an embodied, dynamic way. In the sangoma way, the entirety of my being was used to heal.

## THE MYSTICAL LANDSCAPE OF IRELAND

While reconnecting to my Irish roots as a full sangoma, I now noticed many similarities between the Irish and Xhosa people. For one, they both liked to drink, tell stories, and sing. The people I gravitated to instinctively were musicians. Most of them were also prolific dreamers and had a calling toward music verging on the profound. I found this curious because the word sangoma comes from the isiZulu language and means "person or people (pl.) of the song," or alternatively "person or people (pl.) of the drum." It refers to people who connect with their ancestral spirits through rhythm and song, and I had similar experiences in Ireland.

A good friend, Antoinette, mentored me in Irish traditional music and introduced me to a number of her musical colleagues. I will never forget one evening in an old pub in Ennistymon in the heartland of Irish traditional music. The sun had set and the drinks were flowing. Antoinette introduced me to Ronan, a well-known Irish musician and old friend of hers. He could play various instruments, and that night he specialized in the bodhran, a round Irish drum covered in goatskin and played with a small wooden stick. The musician hits the skin in quick succession, making an unusual sound; to me, it sounded like runaway horses. The musicians sat in a semicircle and Ronan called forth a song in Gaelic. The other musicians nodded their heads in agreement, and the session began. I was transported back into the township with my fellow Xhosa sangomas connecting with the ancestral spirits. I could feel the energy created by the musical vibrations. They were circular, like spirals going higher and higher with each voice, whistle, and drum movement.

At the end of one particular song, Ronan turned to me and said, "Do you play, John?"

I said, "African drumming, but nothing else so far."

He replied, "Ahh, sure, you would do well with the bodhran, then. Sorry I don't have one to spare, but here is one of my sticks. Just bang it on something and join us, okay?"

I accepted his old bodhran stick with mild amusement, and then the session continued and I did as he asked; I banged away on the table. Suddenly I could feel the rhythms more acutely, and when I closed my eyes it was very similar to dancing as a Xhosa sangoma. I felt the presence of my Irish "bone people," my ancestors, moving closer with a nod and a wink, a twist and a turn. The rhythms created a shimmering, transcendent feeling as we pulled our spirits together and took the pub to another place. Time became immaterial and the only language we spoke together was the language of rhythm. Ronan winked, the candles flickered, and I heard a faint popping in my ears, like when you're on a jet climbing above the clouds.

There is no traditional shamanic culture in Europe like there is in South Africa, where people are trained and apprenticed, becoming traditional healers after a lengthy period. Sadly, the ways of the druids and Celtic magicians and sorcerers died out hundreds of years ago due to changing politics and Christianity. Yet I believe nothing is forgotten. All our personal and ancestral memories are stored in our DNA, and we use the memory that is relevant to our lives. I believe that Irish shamanic knowledge moved sideways into Irish traditional music because there are strong parallels between Irish master musicians and sangomas. Ardent traditional musicians often have to learn Gaelic to understand the old songs. And the old songs, like our iingoma, contain great spiritual potency, with the ability to contain portals between the realms of the living and the spirit. When I heard the old Irish songs, I felt the leopard inside me stirring and the vortex energies of my initiations being fed.

## LESSONS LEARNED FROM A SEVEN-YEAR ODYSSEY

During the seven years I led retreats and public talks around the world, I felt privileged to be invited to new communities that wanted to connect more deeply to their ancestors and dreams. Some common themes emerged.

When I taught people how to pray and connect with their bones and spirit, they received amazing ancestral dreams: dreams that connected them to their vital essence, often accompanied by tears and other strong emotions.

When I taught people the importance of saying their forebears' names, at first most people excluded their mother's side of the family. I reminded them of their mother's side, and they had an "aha" moment, with the room taking on a new focus. After one small ceremony in the United Kingdom, a lady told me she hadn't said her mother's family name aloud for at least thirty years. She was deeply emotional about it. This confirmed an idea I'd had for years: that our first point of separation is between male and female. When we can equally revere both sides of our families, we achieve a sense of balance inside. And I believe our first split, or sense of separation, as human beings is along gender lines rather than racial.

I met many challenges, seen and unseen, during my early years of sharing sacred African ancestral teachings. One challenge was facing people's fears and misconceptions around traditional African medicine. People were polite, but I could feel tension in the room when I spoke in isiXhosa. I encouraged people to voice their fears, so they often asked me questions about black magic and voodoo. The early missionaries and colonizers did such a good job of spreading misinformation about African spirituality that more than three hundred years later we still faced this negative stereotype. I dealt with this by assuring people that sangoma and traditional healers like me were solely focused on healing—that if we practiced the "dark arts," we wouldn't be healers. I passed around a little furry African lion as a "talking stick" to encourage group participation, and it worked wonders.

Another challenge I faced was people questioning my authenticity because of my race. During these times, I held up my lineage and personal story as witness to my integrity. I said that I had been called through dreams to become a sangoma from both my own blood ancestors and the Xhosa nation, and that my Xhosa teacher and her husband had invited me to apprentice. When I noticed incredulous looks pass over the audience, I asked if anyone had a problem with Desmond Tutu becoming an Anglican archbishop. No one did—they even seemed annoyed by that question. Back I went to the teachings of Ubuntu: if someone has a calling and demonstrates it with conviction and authenticity, it shouldn't matter what color their skin is or what culture they are from. People seemed to agree with this.

I encouraged people to close their eyes and feel the spirit of Africa I had brought with me. Then when I sang and drummed, they understood something beyond words. Strong emotions frequently surfaced in my workshops and retreats, the release of energy pent up over years of people not listening to their spirits. Sometimes the emotion was joy; often it was grief or anger. At such times, I reminded participants that in Europe people have forgotten to honor their ancestors, something probably not practiced since the time of the druids, at least two thousand years ago.[1]

In South Africa the strength of a ceremony is gauged by the depth of the feelings it stirs—good or bad is immaterial. It is a sign of the umbilini, or core essence of the person being activated. I encouraged people to work through these feelings and try to identify their roots. The release of feelings is a sign that their center is waking up and new life is being created inside them. Like an expectant mother experiencing morning sickness, all life has a bittersweet edge to it. To integrate beauty, we often need to look at the sadness or shadow feelings holding us back. I told people that the only time they should be concerned during my retreats was if they didn't feel anything. If that happened, I said, I would work with them in another way. But, in fact, feelings always came up.

## KEEPER OF THE EARTH SHRINE

My primary function during workshops or ceremonies was to be a shrine keeper, to create a sacred space through which people could dream and connect to their ancestors. One by one, each person knelt down, placed a stick of incense in the earth altar in the center of the room, and said their ancestors' names. It was like hearing prayers to the goddess of nature. By the end of the workshop, they emerged fresh and invigorated. I considered it a success when people dreamed about their ancestors—and this occurred every single time.

My job was to help people identify their ancestral dreams and illustrate the importance of treating them with the right level of respect and purity. People were often oblivious to the power of their own dreams and the unique opportunities and spiritual gifts they offered. Yet as soon as we respect our own dreams and listen to their messages, we receive more. We all possess the capacity to receive prophetic or psychic dreams, but for many people in the Western world it is like a muscle that has atrophied. To strengthen this natural gift, we need to use it. This requires patience, determination, and focus.

Most people found it difficult to relate to me as both John and as the sangoma, for they were like two different personalities. People expected me to be a superman—to not get sick or tired after my retreats. I often explained that my teacher is often sick, as was Zen Master Su Bong.

Being a wounded healer means feeling both your spirit and your vulnerabilities, experiencing your fragility while allowing umoya to move through you. To heal others and the world around you, you need to be kind to yourself, something you achieve through quiet reflection and by witnessing nature and the perpetual movement of life around you.

My sangoma self was strong and self-assured, filled with energy that pulsed and moved. I became the living embodiment of my totem animal. Before I performed a ceremony, I felt the presence of the leopard going through me, waking my senses and stirring my soul. This was always intoxicating. But in keeping with the leopard's message after my initiation—dancing at the corner of my eye and issuing a silent warning—the stronger my ceremonies became, the more difficulty I experienced in daily life. I constantly struggled to balance the two different parts of me: the spiritual and the mundane. Most of the time I was living and working in a Western world with no understanding of traditional shamans like me.

Finally, I learned to balance the dynamic energy of my sangoma spirit with my "John" personality through physical exercise. I brought this lesson into my workshops, stressing the importance of maintaining a good relationship with our bone body, our physical core.

## THE CALL OF THE BLACK BEAR

After a few years of traveling, I returned to South Africa. I awoke one morning from a peculiar dream: I was walking through the snow following a black bear deep into the forest. Every so often the bear looked over his shoulder to see if I was still behind him. I could just make out his footprints in the snow. My whole body shook from the cold. As I woke, my skin was ice cold to the touch while outside the morning temperature climbed high. I was struck with the spirit of calling; I felt the black bear's call but wasn't sure what it meant.

A few months later I attended an herbal conference in England. An American man was giving a talk about herbalism and the traditional Indian spirituality of North America. My skin went cold and I shook involuntarily as visions of the black bear came to mind—yet I was wide awake. After his talk I joined him in a makeshift tent, where he told me that he had Cherokee Indian blood and had been initiated into the Cherokee medicine way. For him and his people, the black bear symbolized the herbalists of North America. He said that according to legend, thousands of years ago when the human race started moving away from nature, some wise men and women became black bears to keep their connection to nature. They did this for their human brothers and sisters so that if they needed help they could call on the bear clan in dreams or through ancient offerings in the forest.

My dream suddenly made sense to me: the bear needed my help. My new American friend offered to host me, and doors soon opened. A major part of my pilgrimage to the Americas, involving Canada, the United States, and Mexico, began.

The night before I flew to the United States for the first time, I was in between waking and sleep. Before me a black bear moved in and out of my awareness. My leopard spirit sniffed at him; there seemed to be an understanding and a sense of collegial respect between two wild ones living in harmony with Mother Earth.

I landed in Boston and stayed with friends in Vermont. My friends told me that black bears had visited their porch literally the day before I arrived, leaving a scent of their wildness for me to track in my dreams. I met some Cherokee medicine people. After I told them about my dreams and calling, they were quick to give me "bear medicine": various roots to eat and drink that the bear was known to use. I was also given fat from the body of a bear. The point of these medicines was to use them to connect more deeply to the spirit of the bear, to understand its call and the message it had for me.

I started giving divinations and plant healings to my American clients. After a few weeks the bear's call took shape and rang like a bell inside my soul. Many of my clients had Indian blood and were in conflict with themselves because they didn't understand their dreams. Although they lived middle-class Western lifestyles, they also had dreams of indigenous people from a previous time in American history. Their spirits were caught in a time warp, and they didn't know how to integrate their dream selves with their current lifestyles. They felt ill at ease and guilty. When I inquired about their feelings of guilt, it was like opening Pandora's box. The black bear from my dreams sniffed the air and rubbed against a nearby tree, and my leopard spirit sat closer to protect me as I heard the sins of humanity.

My clients told me a little bit about their personal history and the history of North America. From the early fifteenth century to the late nineteenth century, millions of North American Indian people were killed by the invading European colonizers—over four hundred years of brutal conflict. The people died from war, murder, or disease. There were even stories of blankets and food being infected with the small-pox virus and then sent down rivers on boats.[2] Moreover, America had enslaved hundreds of thousands of African people. These barbaric acts left scars on the living, some of which I witnessed in my divination room while hearing people's dreams and feeling their connection to their bones and ancestors.

In cases where Indians and African women were raped, the next generation had both victim and perpetrator in their blood. This was true for many of my African American clients. My Ubuntu teachings talk about honoring our ancestors—regardless of whether we think they were right or wrong—so that we can learn to heal the sins of the past. This may seem like magical, wishful thinking but I was fortunate enough to witness its effect.

## RECONCILIATION CEREMONIES TO HEAL THE PAST

At a retreat in South Carolina, a man named Paul shared that he was not proud of his ancestors and didn't feel comfortable having their blood in his veins. He said he was descended from Davy Crockett, who was responsible for the deaths of many Native Americans. It was also pos-sible Crockett had raped Indian women. Paul said he had Indian blood, and it felt like one part of his blood was at war with the other part. His dreams were powerful, with many Native American elders coming to him at night. He felt a deep sense of shame, uncomfortable with who he was because his life was the result of war and possible rape. A few other people nodded their heads in acknowledgment. This presented a powerful opportunity to help heal Paul's ancestors and living descendants.

I asked Paul if he would like to heal this split inside of him. He replied, "Yes!" I asked him to close his eyes and visualize both sides of his family, male and female, and to feel the blood of his Native American and European ancestors in his veins. Then I encouraged him to listen to his heart and take a few breaths in and out, breathing all the way down into his belly. I urged him to go beyond right and wrong and to simply honor his ancestors for giving him the gift of life; I said he was not responsible for the sins of his ancestors but could speak on behalf of them to help heal the pain of the past. If there was just one drop of his bloodline responsible for atrocities toward Indian people or others, he could turn to face the aggrieved ancestors and say he was sorry.

The tears flowed down Paul's cheeks while he shared his remorse over the senseless killing and inhuman treatment by people in his bloodline toward other ancestors inside of him. He asked them to accept his apology. Then, while placing a stick of incense on the earth altar, he asked for forgiveness on behalf of his ancestors who had perpetrated violent deeds. Pandora's box was shaking while my leopard spirit flicked his tail. The room was filled with tears, grief, and ultimately relief that this painful wound could finally be expressed.

Paul was in his fifties and said this was the first time in his life he could accept himself and the ancestors who created him. He finally felt ready to honor all his ancestors. I encouraged him to continue to pray to his ancestors in this way, and said it could take a few prayer sessions for his dreams to change and his sense of guilt to fade. His most important job was to unify his bloodlines. To do that fully, he would need to apologize on behalf of his ancestors who committed aggressive acts toward others. Over time, with committed, heartfelt practice, I believed Paul's inner work would affect his family for future generations as well as his immediate community.

Violence creates a deep ancestral scar, and I believe it is the job of the living to reconcile the past. We can't undo what happened, but we can create a space to witness it quietly and respect our dead. Hopefully, we can then prevent mindless atrocities from happening in the future.

I also led a few reconciliation ceremonies in South Africa with my elders. As the only white man in my Xhosa community, I felt very guilty and sad about the white colonizers' treatment of the Xhosa people. I had to give voice to these feelings so I could move on with my work as a Xhosa sangoma.

One day I sat with my elders in MaMngwevu's divination room. She asked me how I was. I told her I felt sad in my heart. She asked why, and I said I felt sad for how white people had treated Xhosa people, and I felt ashamed to have white skin.

She looked at me with compassion and said I must let it go. "*Abanye abelungu bangcolile, kodwa nabanye abantu abamnyama bangcolile, kodwa hayi bonke.*" (Some white people act badly, but some black people also act badly. Not everyone is bad.) I heard Mama's words but still felt I needed to do something. I gathered my elders together and organized a semiformal ceremony where I spoke in the kraal and apologized on behalf of white people for the undignified way they had treated the Xhosa people. "*Ndithi, uxolo.*" (I say, sorry.) My elders said they understood that I had nothing to do with the way they were treated, and they thanked me for voicing this painful episode in our history.

Every year I went to the United States, and most years I dreamed about the black bear just before the trip. Like the leopard, the bear wavered and danced on the periphery of my awareness. One year the dream changed slightly. I noticed that the black bear had cubs. She introduced them to me. Then to my shock and horror, I noticed they were sick, with drips going into them. They were being held in the forest in special pens to nurse and rehabilitate them. I interpreted the dream as a sign that the people I was visiting in the United States were spiritually sick and that their sickness came from not being connected properly to their bloodlines. They were being nourished and fed through outside sources, but they were not tuning in to their own well of energy.

I carried on with my work, seeing clients and traveling around the United States. I kept feeling the loss of innocent blood in the land. Whenever I visited sacred places that had been frequented by indigenous people, I felt the songs of the dead in the form of a gentle mist of blood and tears. These feelings only got stronger until one day I was asked to speak in Central Park in New York City. The night before, I received visions of Native American people dressed in traditional leather clothes and feathers. A young woman asked me to help the people be remembered—their stories, their pain; how they lived and how they died.

The next day, I went to the gathering in Central Park. A hundred or more people were dancing, singing, and drumming. The leaves in the trees had turned a crisp golden color. The dance of light and shadow through the leaves reminded me of my dream the night before. I wanted to speak in a lighthearted "light and love" fashion, but that is not the job of a sangoma. Our work is about receiving visions and dreams and telling the people so they can live in harmony with their spirits and the natural world. My leopard spirit cavorted in the leaves with the black bear and her sick cubs. He came leaping toward me and entered my spirit with a ferocious growl.

I told the group that it was hard to be a shaman or prophet, especially when we received difficult, painful visions. I explained that this had happened to me the night before, and I asked if they wanted me to share my vision with them even if it might make them uncomfortable. Everyone said yes. I told them I came from the same tribe as Nelson Mandela. I said I could help this group find spiritual freedom—would they like this? Again, everyone said yes.

So I described my visions of the Indian people who had asked me to tell their story. I recounted the genocide that had happened in the United States, horrors that had largely been forgotten by the current generation. I told them that the United States has been at war for hundreds of years since it exterminated the Indian people, and that the only way to stop the energy of war was to honor the first people.

Memorials should be erected for them and songs sung to honor them. There should be reconciliation ceremonies performed with apologies by the living descendants of those known to be instrumental in the atrocities. I said I could feel the tears of the living reflecting in the tears of the dead.

I told them that ever since I started working in the United States, I had felt a baseline of grief and high emotion. Elephants honor their dead, I said. For us to become human in every way, we need to honor our dead and never forget the loss of innocent lives. The people of today's generation shouldn't feel guilty; they should just remember their people.

I asked the group to join me in a few songs and prayers to honor the forgotten ones on the land where we walked in Central Park. I banged my drum, and my leopard spirit roared ferociously. My voice rose to new heights in an attempt to appease the visions of the night before.

After the ceremony, there was silence. My leopard spirit ran off into the nearby maple leaves to play with the black bear. He seemed to have become quite fond of her and protective of her cubs. What a strange sight!

I sighed as I left the group. No one came up to hug me in the typical American way. My friends said they had never seen me like that before and were shocked. Then a young woman approached me who looked just like the young Indian woman from my vision the previous night, with long, dark hair and sallow skin. She thanked me for speaking the words of her heart. Her whole life she had felt the tears of her people but didn't know how to express this sorrow and wondered whether anyone would listen to her. Her voice broke and she had tears in her eyes.

"You must be strong," I said. "Don't worry about the dead—just remember them in speech, song, and prayer."

I noticed the little bear cubs looking stronger. They were playing catch-up with my leopard, who had to run up a tree to get away from them.

During this seven-year period, my prophetic dreams often happened when I was resting in South Africa with my sangoma family. It always felt as if my ancestral spirits were giving me my assignment for the upcoming year: a particular task or pilgrimage to undertake to either heal or balance myself or offer something to another community.

I dreamed of Mexico a few times. The first dream was of a European man in the 1500s who was helping the local Indian people deal with the Spanish conquistadors. In vivid detail, like a video, I saw this man and heard his story. He went to a sacred mountain in Mexico and jumped off it as he ran from the Spanish soldiers. He was desperately trying to save the Indian people and preserve some of their sacred teachings. In the dream, I was told that I needed to climb this sacred mountain.

I was friends with a healer in Mexico and recounted my dream. I drew the mountain, including important details. He confirmed my dream and agreed to take me to this sacred mountain. I climbed it and visited a few sacred pyramids at the same time.

I loved Mexico—it fed my soul. And I returned from there with wonderful stories and a warm heart. Then the spiral of ancient traditional mysticism seemed to twist and turn, taking me to another level. I dreamed of a Xhosa sangoma lady standing between two Mexican Huichol medicine men. The Huichol, a lineage dating back to the Aztecs, were never conquered by outside forces, and retain a sense of dignity and empowered spirituality that is a joy to behold. They still practice their old shamanic religion with a reverence for the spirits of the land.[3] The sangoma lady and the two Huichol medicine men stared at me intensely in the dream.

I woke with a start and went to tell my elders my dream. I felt that the Xhosa lady in my dream was part of my teacher's medicine lineage. My elders agreed with the interpretation. They said the ancestors and Great Spirit were guiding me over the waters to do ceremony with the Huichol people. They were showing me that a relationship could be forged between these two ancient shamanic medicine cultures, the Xhosa and the Huichol. As the messenger or bridge, I was to go to Mexico and develop a relationship with the Huichol medicine people. The rest would be revealed when the time was right. My teacher blessed me and encouraged me to go to Mexico and work with *abantu ababomvu*, "the red people."

The Huichol gave me hope that the old ways of our ancestors were still alive in the world outside Africa. Their intricate ceremonial work was similar to that of the Xhosa people. They too had beads to denote the rank of the medicine person, and they possessed an intimate knowledge of the plant, animal, and dream worlds. When the senior shaman sang during ceremony, he sounded like a bird. He awoke the primal, fecund, ancient possibilities of the forest within me. The African sunset merged with the Mexican jungle, and my leopard spirit merged with the jaguar. The result was an electric feeling of happiness and energy all through my body.

These healers inspired and excited me, teaching me about the boundless energy of the heart and the magic of the natural world. I felt the immortality of the human spirit with all its potential for desire, grief, beauty, and magic. When the shaman gave me an opportunity to sing in isiXhosa and drum during the ceremony in the forest around a fire, my leopard pounced and my tongue clicked. The rhythm of my voice changed. It felt as if I was being initiated into the world of the forest.

Like my other voyages, my pilgrimage to Copenhagen started with a dream. I was in an African traditional healing shop that I have frequented for close to twenty years. I saw shining beings who spoke to me, and then a light like a comet went straight out of the shop toward the north. In my mind's eye I saw the word SCANDINAVIA, and I thought my ancestral spirits were calling me there.

My energy levels had been fading for a while. Living on the road and constantly giving spiritual succor to people was depleting my inner reserves. I sensed that this was going to be my last pilgrimage to connect with my bloodlines overseas. I wasn't sure how it was going to pan out, so I just sat back and let things unravel.

I was invited to Japan a few weeks after my dream, and my travel agent said the best ticket he could get me was via Copenhagen. I informed some friends in Copenhagen that I was stopping by, and they organized a few events for me. I gave a talk at a friend's house and at a Tibetan Buddhist center. My Viking blood was stirred as I rode an Icelandic horse through the Danish forests. Ancient memories were activated when I walked the medieval streets of Copenhagen, hearing the sounds of the Danish language. I finally felt proud in a humble, dignified way to have all these European nations flooding through my veins. The legacy of apartheid had affected me deeply. For too long I had been ashamed to be a white man. I finally accepted my white skin and made peace with my ancestry. Now I felt I could stand tall. There is beauty in the European bloodlines too.

## JAPAN AND THE SACRED RED FOX

I led a few retreats in Tokyo, which felt like an auspicious completion of a circle for me because I had started my spiritual practice with Japanese Soto Zen. I was pleased to be able to give back to a culture that had given me a vehicle to attain harmony during the time I served at 1 Military Hospital.

As I walked down the busy streets of Tokyo, I observed ancient temples with huge wooden statues outside resembling what I thought was some kind of gargoyle. As I entered the temple grounds, I noticed ancient scripture written on wooden plaques hanging from trees. I made a few bows in the customary Buddhist tradition. I noticed beautiful bowls of water with red ribbons hanging above them and to the side. I bowed and clapped my hands a few times. This seemed appropriate. When I observed other people standing quietly, bowing, and clapping their hands, I was pleased that I was observing the correct form.

The wooden walls of the shrine room were covered in old Japanese writing. People stood quietly with their hands in the prayer position resting on their chests. We all stood in silence, together observing the water and the wooden prayer sheets. The only sounds were the cicadas, so loud they blocked out the distant sounds of traffic.

That night I dreamed I was walking through Tokyo's ancient streets. A large red fox walked ahead of me, and roads opened in front of him. The fox seemed to move in a strange circle or maze. I awoke feeling like I had touched the ancient heart of Japan, but I didn't know what it meant.

Over the course of three weeks, I gave divinations, "throwing the bones" for numerous Japanese people, and I had five different interpreters. I felt my Japanese clients were close to their ancestors. I only had to close my eyes and chant in isiXhosa and I would receive visions of their people on the other side. When the interpreters relayed my advice, I was met with a surprising response. Some of my clients burst into tears and nodded their heads. When they left, I had the good fortune of having Japanese spirituality explained to me in depth via the different interpreters.

I told a few clients to make offerings to the water spirits of a high mountain. At that time, I had no idea about the Japanese Shinto faith, the oldest religion in Japan, going back thousands of years. I also had no idea that an important part of Japanese spiritual culture is making offerings to the nature spirits of sacred mountains like Mount Fuji.[4] My interpreter told me I was acting like a Shinto priest and that she would take me to the nearby shrine after work. Then she took me back to the same shrine I had visited the day before and told me the creatures outside guarding the temple were red foxes that open the doorways to the nature spirits.[5]

As in South Africa, my work in Japan was to hold a mirror to my clients and encourage them to continue their old ancestral practices. I gave them faith that their old traditions and spiritual culture were still alive, and I instilled in them the importance of remembering their ancestors and spiritual ways. I noticed great similarities between the sangoma way and the Shinto faith. We both work with the izinyanya, and over my time in Japan I came to a better understanding of this term. "Silent hidden ones," or ancestors, can also mean "nature spirits." In Japan my blond hair and blue eyes worked in my favor because people came to me looking for something different and exotic. But when they heard my spiritual iindaba, they were moved to tears and deeply humbled. Many had ignored their traditions, hoping for the bright lights and excitement of a Western spiritual approach. But when I spoke as their Shinto priests did, they felt the presence of their ancestors speaking through me and it inspired them to delve deeper into their old customs.

Throughout my travels around the world, I saw tremendous similarities between traditional cultures. We Xhosa sangomas see the essence of life as resting with the nature spirits, and in particular the water spirits. So imagine my surprise when during my last week in Japan I learned that one of my interpreters was an assistant to the late Masaru Emoto, an internationally renowned Japanese researcher and bestselling author who spoke and wrote about the magic and mystery of water. Studying water crystals under a microscope for a number of years, he came to believe that human consciousness has an effect on the molecular structure of water. Though he was highly criticized by the mainstream scientific community, he managed to bring water into the spotlight and encourage popular culture to treat it as sacred, demonstrating the unique Japanese gift of marrying traditional beliefs and practices with the modern world.[6]

No matter where in the world I found myself, I continued to dream about South Africa and my traditional sangoma community. The ancestral spirits of my teacher and her husband approached me in these dreams and encouraged me to return home to lead certain ceremonies. Back in my sangoma community, I had lengthy meetings with my elders to describe what I had seen both overseas and in the dreamtime. My ancestral dreams were emphatic and clear, their message always "Tell people to continue to honor their ancestors, and follow their ancient traditions."

The younger members of the community looked up to me because I traveled the world and was well educated. One of my elders told me that my iindaba encouraging people to follow their old ways was making a difference because the younger people listened to me. I could have gone on about the wonders of America or the Western world, but instead I consistently praised the old Xhosa ways and encouraged the young to keep following them.

When I led a retreat in Durban, South Africa, I met a professional middle-class Zulu man, Simphiwe, who asked me an important question. He had been raised Christian in a church that disapproved of traditional ancestral practices and saw them as pagan and superstitious. Yet it was hard for his family to ignore their ancestral practices because many people they knew had traditional healers in their families. So he and his friends went to church on Sundays, but they visited traditional healers in the evenings during the week, feeling ashamed for doing that and conflicted inside. Simphiwe had been taught that to be an educated man in Africa, he had to renounce his traditional ways. "Is it wrong for me to consult traditional healers during the week?" he asked.

I felt his wound. I approached him and said, "Thank you for your question. You have spoken about the elephant in the room. The missionaries did great work in Africa, but they also made a lot of mistakes, and we need to forgive them for that. No person can go into another person's home and tell them what to do. In particular, they cannot tell them to stop honoring their ancestors and traditional culture. We are a great nation of lions, elephants, and leopards. We are the nation of Nelson Mandela, Oliver Tambo, and Steve Biko. These are not small people. We need to be proud to be South Africans and proud to practice our traditional ways."

Later that day, Simphiwe came and gave me a hug—an unusual act in the Zulu culture for someone you have just met. He thanked me in his gentle way, his face shining with relief and gratitude.

Over these several years, as I took The Way of the Leopard teachings on the road, the teachings evolved. To begin with, I simply shared the wisdom that had been passed on to me from my elders from my

many years of training as both a Zen student and sangoma apprentice. However, a sangoma's work is never static. We must be pioneers,
continually exploring the mysteries and subtleties of the original
teachings and—always—listen to our dreams. The spiritual lineages
of Korean Zen and Xhosa sangoma merged inside of me. In a rich
alchemy of ancestral mystery, Zen focus combined with my own
intuitions and visions from the road. I came up with The Way of
the Leopard—mindfulness medicine from Africa. These teachings
came to me in response to an important question ruminating in my
spirit: How can I bring ancient African sangoma wisdom to people
who are not connected to traditional shamanic culture? I saw this
as a way for people everywhere to connect to themselves and the
natural world. I developed teachings of my own, designed to help
people cultivate the leopard warrior spirit within them, unleash their
instinct, remember their ancestors, and heed their dreams.

It has become clear to me that a few of these core practices have
strong and lasting healing effects for people, no matter what country
or culture they come from. Now it is time for me to share them with
you. The Way of the Leopard involves a teaching practice that aligns
people with nature and, thus, with their essential humanity. I call this
"Ubuntu 101."

# 16

# Ubuntu 101 Teachings

A good house needs a firm foundation to be turned into a home. Ubuntu 101 represents a foundation in spiritual practice dedicated to helping any human being rediscover their humanity and thus return home to their true self. Let me begin these teachings with a simple story . . .

In a parallel universe where animals can talk and study philosophy, a sick elephant approached a doctor. "Doctor, Doctor, I am so sick inside, and I have traveled the world to find a cure, but all I feel is empty and my life has no meaning. I have worked with the winged ones and they have taught me to see far. I have worked with the two-legged and they have taught me the wonder of language and this crazy thing called 'Google' and the Internet. I have also worked with the finned ones, the dolphin people, and they have taught me to go with the flow and connect with the waters inside me. I have learned many things, but I still feel empty, and the more I study the sicker I feel."

"Hmm . . . that is very interesting," the doctor said. "Have you thought about working with the elephant people?"

"No, I haven't. What a wonderful idea!" the elephant replied.

*To cure illness all we need to do is look within arm's reach of ourselves.*

For eons the human race has struggled with the question "Why do we live and why do we die?" Existential angst has plagued humanity, inspiring philosophers, artists, and spiritual seekers the world over. This angst seems to be reaching epic proportions, as modern illnesses such as heart disease, depression, and cancer become synonymous with Western civilization. The world appears to be succumbing to chaos and disharmony. Yet the answers we seek for balance and harmony might be found where we all began: in Africa. The crisis in modern life is one of soul loss. We know that in order to cure an illness we need to go to the heart of the matter, the source. This is why we need to go to the ancient wisdom teachings of Africa that speak about the heart, blood, and bones, for therein lie the missing teachings of our planet: how to praise and connect to our ancestors.

Just as a tree constantly communicates with its roots through its sap, so we constantly connect with our DNA through our blood and bones. Our journey begins within our hearts; if we listen carefully, the answers we seek can be found in our blood.

"I am what I am because of who we all are"—that is the essence of Ubuntu. This chapter deals with the foundations of human beings: our bones, ancestors, and connection to Spirit and nature—our humanity. We can realize our humanity through acts of kindness and compassion and by honoring our ancestors through the practices I include here.

Ubuntu is like a circle. As soon as a person decides to discover their humanity—to understand why they are alive, their gifts and destiny, they activate their Ubuntu circle. This activation is akin to the most ancient spiritual practice of alchemy, turning base metals into gold. I began to discover this at seventeen, following my dream in which a woman's voice spoke to me: "John, in order for you to find your destiny, you need to come close to death." After twenty years of reflection, I now understand that to connect with our destiny we must connect with our pain.

The pain of being human opens up a world of empathy toward others. But most of all, when you connect deeply with your *own* pain and distinguish your suffering from the suffering around you, you connect with your own soul. Illness and the suffering it brings teach you how to become more human.

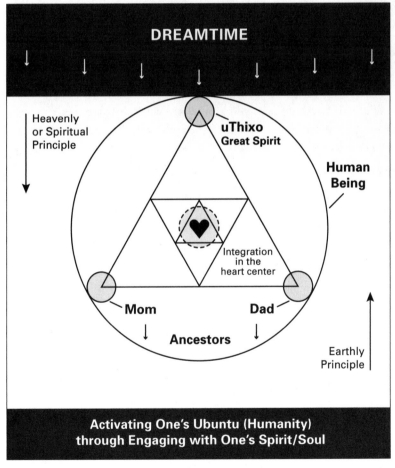

Ubuntu activation map.

To understand our pain, we need to breathe in slowly and learn to occupy our inner world. We need to connect with our destiny and with our soul, the shining incandescent creature within us, and allow it to speak to us. The soul's language is one of images, poetry, and song that speak to us through our dreams and our pain. We need to occupy our inner landscapes, our shadow worlds of longing, greed, sadness, sorrow, and joy, to understand our soul's journey.

Ubuntu teachings describe a system of growing our souls so we are no longer imprisoned by our individual egos but instead expand outward to the larger community. They teach us how to nourish our spirits and reconnect with our hearts. This involves relationship and responsibility. We first need to develop a relationship with ourselves, then with our family, community, and the natural world.

Our spirits are wild, like nature, so think of taming a wild animal, such as a horse or an ox. Only a gentle, firm, and disciplined voice will suffice. If you shout at a wild animal or beat it, it will either run away from you or attack you. Pursue your own soul with calmness and care. Speak gently to it. In doing so, you will water the "tree of life" within you and open the door to your human gifts and destiny.

What is destiny but the pursuit of your dreams, of something that makes you feel alive? Something that makes the electricity, or umbilini energy inside you, pulsate with vigor and vitality. And what will activate your umbilini, or electrical center? The decision to live and follow the call of your heart.

## THE WAY OF THE LEOPARD WARRIOR

I liken the Ubuntu teachings to The Way of the Leopard because to harmonize ourselves with nature we need to look to the animal kingdom. In Southern Africa, the leopard is a totem of traditional healers, or *iinyanga* (herbalists), and sangomas, reminding us humans about the importance of connecting to all our senses and moving through the natural world with harmony, balance, mindfulness, and poise. The leopard represents the most sublime intuitive intelligence the natural world has to offer, inspiring healers, mystics, and artists to keep sensing and feeling on every level. The leopard's sense of smell is especially acute, and interestingly enough, when we sangomas mix herbs, one of the strongest senses we use is smell, for it opens our third eye and helps us merge with the world around us.

To become a leopard warrior, we need to learn to listen to our heart and breathe; to know when to rest and wait and when to stalk and pounce; to move in a mindful way from stillness to action.

## Listening to the Heart

The root cause of sickness is disharmony inside, which filters outward from our inner landscape to the outside world. The warfare and disharmony around our planet today speak to a profound imbalance of the inner world of mankind. It is not surprising, then, that according to the World Health Organization, the leading causes of death in the world are heart disease and stroke.[1] Our inner mental and psychological states can have a profound effect on our physical bodies. To correct this, we each have a responsibility to listen to our hearts.

The heart is the only organ that traverses the physical and metaphysical worlds. It is the master of the human being. The mind is not the master because the mind has no substance. Rather, the mind is the natural servant of the heart and helps carry out instructions through thought, feeling, intuition, and images.

## Following the Breath

Too often we have a fascination with the outer world, evident in social media like Facebook. The aim of "leopard medicine" is to occupy our inner landscapes, to rediscover our "soul's book," or inner face, the book of life within us. In sangoma divination, we connect with our umoya, and our focus is *ukuvula incwadi*, "to open the book." Through connecting deeply to our inner spirit, we can help the world.

Close your eyes and follow your breath toward your inner landscape. Allow the breath to move like a river down toward your belly. Take three deep breaths, moving your awareness toward your toes. Become aware of your heartbeat. Breathe into your heart. Notice how it is beating. Accept your own rhythm. Continue to breathe into your heart, feeling the subtle vibrations in your hands, feet, and chest. Breathe deeply.

Now dive into your inner landscape, becoming more aware of thoughts, emotions, images, and feelings. Just notice them. Breathe. As the breath moves through this inner world, difficult, unruly thoughts, feelings, and emotions may emerge. If you have disturbing thoughts or emotions, don't worry. Emotions are like clouds moving across the sky. We all have them—they're all part of the gift of being human. Recognize and acknowledge them. Then, as the breath moves through the body, you will learn to consciously occupy all the shadow, or unacknowledged parts, of yourself. Breathe deeply into your heart. How is it feeling now? Notice what happens with a mindful awareness of the breath.

Become aware of the power of your breath and how you can change your emotions by simply elongating your breath or just holding it for a few moments in the pit of your belly. Make a decision to become more mindful in your life and to consciously change patterns or habits that are not serving you. As you control your breath, so you learn to control aspects of your life. This builds confidence, self-esteem, and ultimately happiness.

## ACTIVATING YOUR UBUNTU: THREE PRACTICES TO HELP YOU UNCOVER THE MYSTERY OF WHAT IT MEANS TO BE A HUMAN BEING

I have devised some simple practices to help people find their life calling and activate their Ubuntu. Yet how this unfolds depends on the intention of the seeker—the harder the practice, the deeper the reward. Being born with a psychic or intuitive gift is just the beginning. My beloved teachers, including Zen Master Su Bong and MaMngwevu, worked exceptionally hard to realize their life's calling. Their dreams served as a mere prologue. Our task is always to merge our hopes and dreams with our lived reality. Then we can find inner harmony and spread its fragrance around the world. Like the lotus flower blossoming in full summer, its buds in springtime are just half the story.

These practices form the foundation of my Ubuntu 101 teachings. You can perform them daily or a few times a week. In terms of time commitment, less is more, so if you are struggling with a busy schedule, I recommend a daily heartbeat practice over a cup of tea.

Ubuntu 101 involves three dynamic mindfulness processes: connecting with your heartbeat and feeling your soul stirring within; praying to your ancestors and connecting with your blood and bones; and the art of dreaming and becoming aware of your inner landscape. Before you start these simple practices, it will be helpful to create a sacred space and do some cleansing.

> *Create a sacred space.* Find a room or quiet space in your home to do your practices in, and tidy it up. You will need a comfortable cushion or chair. If you can, open a window and light some incense to freshen the air.

> *Do a physical cleanse.* Especially if you are feeling a bit heavy or down emotionally, a physical cleanse is beneficial. You can perform this cleanse before you do these practices for the first time, and then do it whenever you are feeling low in energy or fatigued. Start by smudging.
> Living in South Africa as I do, I do this with white sage or impepho. If you don't have these herbs, you can use good-quality incense.
> Take the lighted sage or incense and move it slowly around the body. Pay attention to the key energy centers: the crown of your head, back of your neck, throat, heart, solar plexus, below your navel, lower back, arms, and legs. Spend some time moving the smoke over your hands and under your feet. Become aware of your thoughts. Keep your intention clear with a positive affirmation: "I am cleansing my body to remove unwanted energies, whether they are from my own mind, other people, or my environment."
> After you smudge, place a tablespoon each of organic sea salt and Epsom salts into a bath of warm water. Lie in the

bath and scrub from head toe with a cloth. Don't use any soap or shampoo. Now you are ready to begin your practice.

## ◎ PRACTICE 1  Heartbeat Meditation

To prepare for the heartbeat meditation, find a blanket that has a color and texture you love and makes you feel warm and fuzzy inside. Next, make a warm cup of herbal tea; select one that aids your body and mind. Add a bit of organic honey to sweeten and nourish your heart (unless sugar presents a health problem for you).

Bring your blanket and tea to your sacred space, and sit comfortably on a cushion or in a chair. Set your tea at arm's reach. Keep your back straight, not ramrod or stiff—you need to feel the natural curve of your lower back. Feel your spine moving naturally upward toward the sky. Wrap yourself in your blanket.

Instead of giving yourself a time period in which to meditate, such as fifteen or twenty minutes, decide you will sit down over a cup of tea and listen to your heartbeat. If you sit much longer than it takes to drink the tea, that is a bonus. The trick here is not to push yourself to practice.

Take a sip of warm tea before you begin, and remember to sip your tea as you continue to listen to your heartbeat.

1. Close your eyes and take a deep breath, breathing all the way into your belly. Feel your belly expand as you breathe in and move toward your spine as you exhale. Keep your spine straight but relaxed, and let go of any tension in your shoulders, face, and hands. Relax your jaw and keep your teeth slightly apart with your tongue resting behind your upper front teeth.

2. Bring a slight, even mischievous, grin to your face—this will help keep your face open. Now continue with two

more deep breaths. Welcome the breath in like an old friend. Be aware of your thoughts and emotions but don't get attached to them; instead, see them as clouds moving through the sky. Most importantly, don't judge yourself. Be gentle with yourself. Accept yourself. Acknowledge that you are doing your best.

3. Now feel your heartbeat, your pulse, and breathe into it. If you can't feel it, place your index and middle finger on your opposite wrist at the base of the thumb. Concentrate. Now you should be able to feel it, but don't worry if you can't feel it straight away.

4. Sink into your heartbeat. Become aware of the pause between each beat. Breathe into it. Let go. Surrender. Allow your heartbeat to lead you. Accept it. Notice how it is beating: slow, fast, strong, faint. Direct your breath into each beat. If your mind is showing you a story or dramatizing your life, just observe this and then go back to your breath and follow your heart. Your heartbeat will help focus you and increase your mindfulness. If you find that you are falling asleep, half open your eyes and focus a few feet in front of you on the floor. Rest your eyes there.

5. Enjoy your heartbeat. Ride each breath like surfing a wave. Become aware of the rhythm of your heart. The blanket will help you relax and move deeper into your inner landscape. Enjoy the rhythm.

In the sangoma tradition, our first task is to connect with our own spirit, or soul. So, ever so gently, ask yourself silently, "Where is [say your name]?" For instance, I would say, "Where is John?" Then ask yourself, "How are you?"

Gradually, the heartbeat meditation practice will become easier for you and more joyful. Your heart will benefit enormously from your mindful breathing and conscious focus. If you notice yourself becoming emotional after you practice, don't worry. This is a good sign that the practice is working and your spirit is waking up.

## PRACTICE 2 Ancestral Prayer— Connecting with Your Blood and Bones

To do this practice at home, you will first need to create an ancestral altar.

Purchase some ordinary pipe tobacco and find a round wooden or ceramic bowl. Go outside, stand, and say the following aloud: your name, married name (if you are married), your mother's maiden name, your father's name (last name or surname), and any other initiated names you might have received. For instance, "My name is Mary Elisabeth Smith [married name], McAdams [mother's maiden name], Connolly [maiden name, or father's surname]."

Next, say aloud, "I honor and praise the Great Spirit [or use the term of your choice: God, the Great Dreamer, the Creator] and all my ancestors and spirit guides in this world and the next."

Now, sprinkle some tobacco on the ground as an offering and say, "I ask if I may take some soil to be used for my ancestral altar." Listen carefully. If you feel that you shouldn't take soil from a particular place, try another "power spot" or a place in nature that has meaning for you. Sprinkle some more tobacco. Gather some soil and place it in the bowl. Say, "Thank you" aloud, and sprinkle some tobacco for the third time.

You are now ready to do the ancestral prayer.

1. With the bowl you have consecrated with soil, go inside to the sacred space you have created and start your

ancestral practice. It is a good idea to do this part of the
practice kneeling on the floor; this facilitates the spirit of
*thobeka* (humility). Place a yoga mat or rug on the floor
to protect your knees. (If kneeling is uncomfortable, you
can sit in a chair.)

2.  Light a stick of incense and a white candle. This will help
    focus your mind.

3.  Kneel on the ground and, while holding the incense, say
    your name. It is important to use your voice and to
    speak from your heart. As a suggestion, you can say the
    following:

> "I honor and praise the Great Spirit [or God, the
> Great Dreamer, or the Creator]. I honor and
> praise my mother and her people. [Say her family
> name.] I honor and praise my father and his
> people. [Say his family name.] I honor and praise
> my husband [or wife]. [Say their family name(s).]
> I honor and praise my teachers who have taught
> me sacred ways that have benefited my life."

Here you can mention any teacher who has helped you. In
traditional sangoma practice, we mention sangoma teachers
to honor them for guiding us and to help connect us with
their medicine lineage. This practice of honoring our elders
helps to foster dignity and humility. It is fine and correct if
you want to mention me and my Xhosa elders because I am
teaching you this practice. Now say:

> "I ask the Great Spirit and all my ancestors to
> please open the road for me so I can see clearly,
> speak clearly, and walk clearly. So I can realize
> my destiny in this world and the next."

4. Place the incense into the bowl you have consecrated with soil. If you have a wish or something that you need help with, open your heart and speak to your ancestors. This is the oldest form of therapy. Its power is in its simplicity, in speaking from the heart, and in being close to the ground. Finally, close your eyes and listen to your heartbeat. Feel the resonance of your prayers.

5. Now get up and put the bowl in a special place in your home. Each time you want to connect with your ancestors, you can place a stick of incense in the bowl, light a white candle, and kneel on the floor. You can also place a small glass of water on your altar. And on special family days—such as anniversaries, birthdays, or the anniversary of the passing of a loved one—you can place some flowers or special food on your ancestral altar.

*Please take note:* You are honoring and praising your mother, father, and ancestors because they have given you the gift of life. You are *not* honoring and praising bad behavior. It is important to separate personality from consciousness. By connecting with your ancestors in this way, you are connecting with your blood and bones: your DNA, or the tree of life inside you. Be aware of any emotions or feelings that are triggered. Many people can experience profound grief when praying to their ancestors like this because their ancestors have been forgotten for generations, if not hundreds of generations. You nourish your ancestors when you pray in this way. You also nourish your own spirit, or soul, enabling it to grow and rise like a plant reaching for the light.

PRACTICE 3  The Art of Dreaming —
Becoming Aware of Your Inner Landscape

In traditional South African culture, dreams are an essential
part of everyday life. Our soul, or spirit, is seen to connect
with us through our dreams, keeping us in alignment with
our earth walk and day-to-day lives. If someone doesn't
remember their dreams, they are seen as being out of balance
with the world around them because they don't know what
is happening to their soul. Thus, they could potentially
put themselves or their community in harm's way. In these
situations, it is considered crucial that they consult with
a sangoma, who doctors the person's soul and helps them
maintain harmony between the ancestral/spirit world and
temporal reality. To bring the person back into balance, the
sangoma will prescribe herbs for them to wash with and
drink, as well as a ceremonial or prayer practice to help
them connect with their ancestral spirits. As a sangoma, I
am doctoring you, the reader, with my instructions in
this chapter on how to maintain and develop a healthy
relationship with your soul, or spirit, thus supporting both
your relationship to your ancestors and your collective
Ubuntu and life as we know it.

As we become more conscious of our dreams, we become
more conscious of our waking lives. We are also preparing
ourselves spiritually for our final sleep, when we die and leave
our bodies. We come from the Great Dreamer, or Cosmic
Consciousness, and we enter this physical world through
the portal of our mother and father. That is why we honor
them and our ancestors. When we sleep, part of us is always
connected to the Great Dreamer and our original home.

When I experience profound dreams, it feels as if I am
getting a download of information from another place, one
that I am deeply familiar with. Such dreams fill me with
wonder, nourishment, and peace, and this is why I feel
compelled to share this knowledge with others. No matter

how impoverished, abusive, or constricted your material reality might be, your spirit can fly like an eagle when you sleep and help you find answers to your earthly troubles.

### Levels of Dreams

There are three levels of dreaming. The first level reflects your everyday life. You might dream about shopping for clothes or food, for example. There appears to be no meaning to such dreams. It is as if your mind is simply relaxing and replaying what you did during the day.

The second-level dream involves your psychological or emotional self. You might replay an old love or difficult relationship or traumatic experience. If these dreams repeat over years, this might indicate an emotional block, and some form of therapy in which your dreams are recognized and your emotions get a chance to be released in the waking state may help you move forward with your life.

The third level involves prophetic, mystical, or teaching dreams: *amaphupha amhlophe* (white dreams). These are the dreams of sangomas, mystics, and shamans. Everyone gets these dreams to a lesser or greater extent throughout their lives. The trick is to recognize them because they will help you realize your life path. All callings are equal. A plumber is just as important as a shaman, a doctor, or a priest. The most important question is, What is your dream and how is it calling your spirit?

You can identify these prophetic or calling dreams in a number of ways. The most direct approach is through the body. When I experience these dreams, my body feels filled with electricity. I am hyperaware upon awakening. I might also feel abundant and wealthy, as if I have touched gold or God. I feel expansive. Another way to recognize these dreams is by noticing how many of your senses are engaged in the dream. Can you smell fragrances, see colors, hear sounds? What can you perceive? I often experience these dreams with a white or pale-blue background. There might also be other colors present.

Notice the landscapes of these powerful dreams. Do you dream about deserts, forests, the sea, rivers, urban environments, animals, or people? Your dream is saying something about you and your family. Its landscape can depict your ancestry. If your people came from the desert, even if you live elsewhere, it would make sense for you to dream about deserts.

While I was brought up in South Africa, when I started my traditional apprenticeship I dreamed about Ireland and a kind of sea not found off South Africa. I felt my Irish ancestors calling me, so I went to Ireland and saw that the sea was exactly as it appeared in my dreams. Thus, I fulfilled the calling in my dreams, and this made room for other dreams and other callings.

To dream is not enough. If we want our lives to change and our spirits to grow, we must act on our dreams. Our dream lives and our waking state feed and nourish one another.

### How to Receive Prophetic, Mystical Dreams

Dreams are a gift. Never expect to receive a gift. Every time you receive a powerful dream, thank the universe, the Great Spirit, the Great Dreamer, the Creator, or the Great Mother and your ancestors. The act of thankfulness will breed humility; humility will breed good dreams.

It is important to remember and learn from your most vivid dreams and the omens they portend.

### Suggestions to Aid Dream Recall

The first step to remembering your dreams is to look at how you sleep. Do you sleep enough? The average adult needs about six to eight hours of sleep a night. It's good to have at least one morning a week when you leave your alarm off and allow your body to rest deeply. This is one of the easiest ways to remember your dreams. Also, be mindful of how you spend your time two hours before bedtime. Using a computer or mobile device can make it harder to fall asleep and dream.

Before sleep, meditate and do some heartbeat meditation practice either in your sacred space or a similar space that elicits a sense of calmness and peace for you. My journey started with meditating at least twenty minutes a night— this did wonders for my dream recall. However, don't expect anything from your meditation practice. Do it for the love of it and the sheer joy of listening to your heartbeat.

Nutritional supplements like vitamin B complex and magnesium have been known to help with dream recall. However, nothing can compare with good rest and sleep.

If you have a busy and demanding life and poor dream recall, make a decision to remember your dreams. Then make a few practical changes in your life. Turn your computer (and other screens) off at least two hours before bedtime. Instead, read a book. Take a long bath and add essential oils such as lavender, frankincense, or rosemary to the water. You can also add about two tablespoons of Epsom salts. Do this for at least three consecutive nights.

Buy a beautiful dream journal. Keep it by your bedside at night. When you first wake up, before doing anything else, open your book and write the first thing that comes to mind. Don't worry if it is silly or doesn't make sense. Note your emotions and any images and colors that come to mind. Remembering an emotion or feeling from the dream state is a good start.

When you write your dreams down, give them a theme such as "Dragon's Breath" or "Magic Mountains," or whatever your imagination creates. Also, note where you had the dream—at home, when traveling, or at a friend's house, for example. Noting themes and locations will help you track and make sense of your dreams. Also, put a date to your dream. Over time, you can look back on your dreams and gain another picture of your inner world.

Never expect to remember your dreams, but always give thanks when you do! In a subtle way you are connecting with a deeper part of yourself, and ultimately with the Great Dreamer and where we all come from.

Our dreams are like giant mandalas, with each dream connecting to another. It is common to have all three dream levels in one dream because we dream in a spiral or a circle, never in a straight line, because the nature of our indigenous soul is more magical than we can truly believe. To be indigenous means to think and feel from the heart and to constantly receive guidance from the dream world. Remember, "*Uthando luthando, ubunto luthando.*" (Love is love, humanity is love.) Our journey is to occupy our inner landscapes and mine the love therein.

## THE PRACTICES IN SUMMARY

The practices described in this chapter are your portal into The Way of the Leopard warrior. You can perform all three of them daily. How long does it take you to drink a cup of tea? You can spend that amount of time closing your eyes and delving into your inner world while listening to your heartbeat. You can write your dreams down upon waking or before you sleep at night. I usually write mine down before I sleep, then do some simple ancestral prayers on my knees, and end with a heartbeat meditation practice. Just ten to twenty minutes a day will reap huge rewards in developing more inner peace. But try not to look at your watch. See it like surfing. Enjoy your breath and heartbeat and let them teach you about your own inner nature.

My wish for you is that over time you become more intuitive, more awake, and will experience renewed joy and happiness in your daily life.

# Epilogue

The teachings I have shared are a radical form of mindfulness from Africa. Because they are so simple, I often refer to them as "African Zen." We listen to our own hearts, without judgment or opinions, hearing the beating in our chests in the same way we observe the sounds of ocean waves. Over time, this results in profound appreciation and love, for there is nothing more reassuring to a child than the sound of the mother's heartbeat, whether in the womb or outside it. Then we stoke the fire of our Ubuntu by honoring our ancestors and giving thanks for the gift of life inside us. Finally, we listen to our dreams as indicators of our connection to our soul, for this is the human journey, regardless of race, creed, or gender.

The world as we know it now is very sick. The planet is heating up, and we face political and social turmoil at every turn. The question is, What can we do to turn things around, to create more harmony and happiness for mankind and the natural world?

Physicians and healers from time immemorial have known that to cure a disease we need to take some small part of it and make a healing elixir from it. The antidote to a poisonous snakebite contains minute quantities of snake venom. A similar idea is seen in homeopathy, a healing system based on the doctrine of "like cures like."

The rampant destruction of the natural world, which then places untold stresses on governments and people, is being caused by the materialistic Western lifestyle, an ever-expanding cycle of buying and consuming—this is our sickness. At the heart of this disease is the cultlike focus on the individual. Yet therein lies the good news, the secret to the healing tincture. If individual action is what drives the consumerist engine that is making us sick, the same spirit of the individual can repair and restore harmony to our world.

People think that social revolutions start with charismatic leaders, but this is not correct. Social movements begin when ordinary individuals set aside their differences and petty jealousies and perceive the humanity that binds them. When they decide to become warriors and stand up for what they believe in, everything is possible. I witnessed the worst form of social engineering in South Africa during apartheid—and I also saw it fall. Most people think it was Mandela who overthrew the apartheid regime, but they are wrong. It was ordinary South Africans who recognized the injustice around them and stood up for their own dignity and the dignity of their forefathers and mothers.

Another force is also at work in the sickness of our world: radical forgetfulness. People are no longer connected to their ancestors, and as they lose touch with their forefathers and the memories of their people, they also lose touch with their spiritual gifts and intrinsic humanity. To stem this tide of forgetfulness, people need to become like warriors and make a decision to wake up on every level, from their bones and cells to the whispers of their dreams at night.

Empowering the individual to perceive and nurture ubunzulu bobuntu—the depth of humanity—is what The Way of the Leopard is all about. It is about us as individuals engaging with our lives with greater clarity so we may perceive our gifts and their power and put them to use, joining with the rest of humanity in restoring balance to our ailing world.

A leopard warrior is a spiritual soldier who mirrors the natural world and directs their gaze inward to answer the call of their spirit. Important questions to meditate on are "Why am I alive?" and "How is nature calling me?" Mindful practices of listening to the heart, honoring our bones (ancestors), and observing our dreamtime help crystalize the call of umoya—the wind, or soul/spirit inside of us. What helps us with these practices is the meticulous observation of nature. The birds know what their job is. The elephants move through the African savannah as if directed by a hidden conductor orchestrating their movements with a subtle harmony infused with intelligence and wonder. Human beings also have this ability to move with grace and beauty—when they are awake.

A leopard warrior is someone who has decided to wake up and take action, to activate their Ubuntu—to listen to the call of their spirit, sometimes manifested in dreams, and take the necessary steps to do what is being asked of them.

Very often, illness plays a role in this. It is a powerful conduit for spiritual transformation. I believe all illnesses are a call for people to look at their inner lives and strive toward harmony in some form. This always requires making behavioral changes. To be a leopard warrior means to feel our suffering and take the necessary steps to ameliorate it. Often, this suffering lies at the core of our spiritual gifts. We cannot be afraid of the shadow inside of us. We must learn to dance with it like the leopard moves through the twilight.

All war is a manifestation of the inner war between the mind and the heart. As we make peace within ourselves, all life benefits. In meditating on our hearts, our wounds become evident, and it is very important that we learn to accept what we find there.

In my experience traveling the world, I have observed that many people in the Western world suffer low spiritual self-esteem. The way to heal ourselves is to accept ourselves and what we bring to the world. I am proud to be a blond-haired, blue-eyed traditional sangoma, although many people I meet struggle with that combination. Life is full of contradictions and paradoxes. Africa can teach the Western world and the Western world can teach Africa. Spiritual emancipation is about opening our hearts and helping one another.

Some of my ancestors were bankers, doctors, and farmers. I've been called to become a sangoma to help people honor their ancestors and nurture the mystical side of their natures. Part of my training and teaching is about going beyond the limitations of our conditioned mind. I look forward to the day when the world doesn't think a white-skinned traditional sangoma is any stranger than a black-skinned African Anglican priest. We all have the responsibility to bridge the divide between perceived differences of color, culture, or gender. Part of waking up and being grateful for our humanity is accepting one another for our gifts and recognizing the red blood that binds us all.

Ultimately, a leopard warrior is a tracker—a tracker of the soul and the body, of dreams and nature. And what is tracking but looking at patterns, the patterns of the world and of nature. How do these patterns make us feel? How do they make us move? How do they make us think?

Though the practices I teach are simple, becoming a warrior is not easy. It requires great faith in our instincts and our ability to feel deeply and passionately. It requires trusting in the power of nature to hold us at every moment. To do this authentically means to feel all the way down to our inner being, to our bones, to accept our feelings without judgment or criticism: complete acceptance—100 percent. And then we stand tall and make the next move.

A leopard warrior is someone who feels deeply, stands strongly, and commits to a cause they believe in. They act from their bones and from their heart, from the innermost core of their being. And often these actions come from a deep place of spiritual calling. This is a pure, noble place. It is a place of altruism, of Ubuntu. And one of its salient characteristics is always helping others. When we speak from this deep "bone" place inside of us, it is no longer the egoic, selfish spirit that speaks but a spirit that is open to the world.

A leopard warrior maintains a sense of dignity, resolve, and inner purpose by connecting to the fire and wind of their inner life-force energy, their umoya, and tracking the subtle fragrances that linger in the peripheries of the spirit. If you dream something and feel your heart and soul being called from a deep place, listen to the call of that dream. This will move you in the direction of the leopard warrior. As you do it more courageously, you will learn to believe in yourself and your life will change. As with dancing, as you change a small pattern or rhythm, nature and the people around you will in turn dance to another rhythm—the rhythm of authenticity, the rhythm of truth.

The rhythm of truth. These words rang in my ears as I recently tracked an elephant through the bush while on safari in South Africa with a group. The pungent smell of the early morning grasses permeated my senses and energized my spirit. Suddenly a young bull elephant appeared in front of us. The elephant danced! It moved its body quickly from side to side, speaking the rhythmic language of nature.

I felt we were connecting to an ancient wisdom keeper from a forgotten time. We spoke gently to it for a few moments. Then it lifted its front legs and pivoted like a ballerina, shook its head from side to side, and walked casually away into the bush. We moved ahead in eager anticipation of what we might witness next. Moving like the leopard through the African bushveld, listening with all our senses and following with an open heart.

# Acknowledgments

In the spirit of Ubuntu, this book owes its creation to a community of people. I thank my elders for their support and encouragement, including my lovely parents, Yonnie and Peter Lockley; my teacher MaMngwevu; Tat' uSukwini; and Tat' uBongani. Words can't express my gratitude and thanks to you completely. Tat' uBongani has been my advisor, friend, and mentor for many years, helping me bridge the Western world and Xhosa traditional culture with grace and dignity. *Enkosi, Tata!* (Thank you, father!) My friend Sidney Peter introduced me to MaMngwevu, spent hours teaching me isiXhosa, and helped me navigate the beauty of Xhosa culture. Sadly, Sidney, a proud Xhosa man who greatly loved his people and his family, died a few years ago. This is for you too, Sid, and your family. *Masiy' embo, amasiko amadala!* (Let us remember the old cultural ways!)

I would like to thank all the skilled and wonderful sangomas both in the Eastern Cape and around South Africa. I honor you and your dedication in holding the flame of generations of sangomas before you. Credo Mutwa, thank you for your teachings and eldership. You have inspired me for years and taught me the importance of connecting with the bones. I feel honored to have spent time with you and learned some of the mystical ways of Africa.

I have been blessed with friends in many countries who have hosted me and encouraged me to write this book. Your kindness helped facilitate my teachings. To my friends in the United Kingdom, including Felicity Wright and Richard Pantlin, and Jez Hughes for his words of wisdom around dreams, writing, and the publishing process and for nudging me to get my work published. Also Sally Turner for her support with publicity and helping me get my voice into the world. The vision of this book started as a conversation between us in 2009. Thank you, Sally, for helping make this dream possible for me!

In Ireland a special thank-you to Henry Rowan for his support and guidance. He encapsulates the Irish spirit for me of gentility, wisdom, and great humor. Also my friends Keith Grainger and Miriam

Donoghue, Noelle Joyce, Duncan Barrett, Julien Joly, Sandra Nolan, Liam Flaherty, and others. Seamus Cashman, a hearty thank-you for helping me navigate the complicated world of publishing. Liam O'Maoli for his input on Irish folk music. The Dancing the Rainbow teachers, Lani O'Hanlon and Antoinette Spillane: thank you for opening the road of Irish music and mysticism for me. Sadly, Antoinette Spillane died a few years ago, but her love and mentorship will continue to live in my heart.

Thanks to Julie Beet and her husband, Eliot Mitchell, for supporting me in Vermont and helping me to get my voice out in the United States. And a community of organizers and host families including Pati Turner from the Sacred Earth Foundation in Colorado; Carol and Tony Asiaghi for support in New York City; Cindy McGinley in Syracuse, New York; Jan Engels-Smith and her Lightsong community; and Laurrien "La" Gilman in Portland, Oregon. And a big thank-you to Elenore Snow for driving me through the Colorado mountains and assisting me with my audition at Sounds True's studios.

Special thanks to my academic friends at my old alma mater, Rhodes University. Professor Julie Wells for her assistance on colonialism in the Eastern Cape. Dr. Penny Bernhard for her friendship, support, and guidance on current sangoma literature and research. Dr. Hleze Kunju for making sure that my isiXhosa writing is acceptable to my fellow isiXhosa speakers. *Enkosi, mhlobo wam.* (Thank you, my friend). And Craig Foster, for sharing his stories with me about his remarkable experience with Bushmen trackers in the Kalahari desert, Botswana.

My Zen friends, teachers, monks, nuns, and masters, I salute you! Deep bows to all of you! From Onesan, my first Zen teacher, to Zen Master Su Bong, Zen Master Seung Sahn, and Antony and Margie Osler. Antony and Margie, you hold the flame of the Zen dharma in South Africa for me—thank you for your love and support. Zen Master Su Bong's words and guidance will ring like a Tibetan bowl inside of me for eternity. Thank you, sir! And thank you, Zen Master Seung Sahn, for welcoming me into your army of Zen monks. Although I declined your offer to join you, deciding to become an African monk instead, part of me continues to walk with you. *Kamsamida!* (Thank you!) Also a special thank-you to Charlotte Jefferay for your friendship and for holding a beautiful meditation space in your home for over twenty years. What a gift you have offered the world!

I would like to acknowledge and thank all those people who touched my life and whose names I changed for privacy. Although your names have been changed, the message and stories you shared with me will continue for as long as my story is read. I hope my words will bring you many blessings.

To all those wonderful souls who have endorsed my work, thank you! A special thanks to Itzhak Beery, Charlie Morley, Sandra Ingerman, Hank Wesselman, Robert Waggoner,

I wish to thank all the soldiers at 1 Military Hospital, Voortrekkerhoogte, South Africa whose courage in the face of adversity set me on my healing journey; and to my uncle, Colonel (retired) Richard Lockley, for teaching me about the dignity of soldiers.

A special mention of thanks to my colleague and friend Malidoma Somé, who wrote such an encouraging foreword and suggested I get in touch with Sounds True.

Some of the photographs were taken by skilled journalists who managed to capture the mood and atmosphere of my traditional ceremonies. Special thanks to Dianne Tipping-Woods and Kanina Foss.

A huge thank-you to Seyta Selter, my research assistant, project manager, and friend. And the Sounds True community of mystics, writers, and teachers. I feel honored to be part of your community. And special thanks to Sheridan McCarthy, my editor, who mentored me through the remarkable process of editing this book. Also Jennifer Brown for believing in me and inviting me to perform at Sounds True Studios one clear day in October 2015. Everything flowed from then on.

And to all my clients and students who have shared their stories and hearts with me: this book is for you! Thank you! And finally, to you, the reader. Thank you for taking the time to read this story. I pray that it will inspire you and help to open your road.

# Gratitude Speech

It is customary for a sangoma to thank his elders, ancestors, and community. As this book is a testament to indigenous healing and thus is like a ceremony, it is appropriate for me to end with my nqula, or praise speech. Indigenous healing arts are threatened by Western culture and technology, which is why I think it is vital to honor the wisdom keepers of our human family. My Xhosa elders represent this, and I pray their ways will always be remembered, loved, and appreciated.

I have traveled all over this world, such places as Australia, England, Ireland, Germany, and France, and all over South Africa. In all these places, I have not seen or felt the connection to the ancestors that I have felt here in the Eastern Cape.

Ladies and gentlemen, be proud of your culture and customs.

You are lucky and rich in spirit. You have no money, but you are connected to your ancestors.

When you sing and dance you raise the spirits of all of our ancestors, our collective human family. I tell people overseas that here in South Africa we have gold in the form of the sangoma culture.

The world is dying, my friends. In Europe and throughout the Western world, people have forgotten the old ways of living. The world is dying because of greediness and a lack of humanity.

You give hope because here I receive the depth of humanity through sangoma teachings. Wherever I am in the Eastern Cape, I feel the presence of humanity.

Fathers and mothers, don't forget to teach your children your culture and customs!

When you do spiritual work honoring your ancestors in the Eastern Cape, you send a light throughout South Africa and the world.

You give people hope. Thank you so much!

## *Iindaba ZikaCingolweendaba*
(John's "spirit news" translated into isiXhosa)

Ndihambile phantse umhlaba wonke, Australia, England, Ireland, Germany, France noMzantsi Afrika wonke. Kuzo zonke ezi ndawo, eRhini kulapho ndiqhagamshelana khona nezinyanya nangakumbi. Mawethu! Zingceni ngenkcubeko yenu. Ninethamsanqa nobutyebi bomoya. Aninamali, kodwa niqhagamshelene nezinyanya zenu. Xa nicula nixhentsa, nichukumisa umoya wabaphantsi, kwakunye noluntu luphela. Ndiyabaxelela abantu baphesheya ukuba apha eMzantsi Afrika sinayo igolide eyiyinkcubeko yamaGqirha. Bahlobo bam, ilizwe liyatshabalala. Abantu baseNtshona bayilibala indlela endala yokuphila. Ilizwe liyatshabalala, ngenxa yokunyoluka nokungabinabuntu.

Bazali ze ningakulibali ukufundisa abantwana benu ngamasiko nezithethe! Xa nisenza imisebenzi yokuthobela izinyanya apha eMpuma Kapa, niba sisikhanyiso eMzantsi Afrika nakwilizwe liphela.

Ninika abantu ithemba. Enkosi kakhulu!

# Notes

## PROLOGUE

1. *Sangoma* is a colloquial term derived from the isiZulu words "isangoma" (singular) and "izangoma" (plural). It is commonly used to refer to all kinds of diviners in Southern Africa. These are people who have an ancestral calling and, in answering this call, have undergone (sometimes lengthy) apprenticeships involving dream work, dancing, drumming, and medicinal plants. When they complete their apprenticeship, they have the ability to work with ancestors through trance dancing, dreams, and divination. Traditional herbalism is considered different unless the healer has been called by their ancestors and undergone an apprenticeship focusing on ancestral communication. Flint, *Healing Traditions*.

## INTRODUCTION

1. South African History Online, "Vusamazulu Credo Mutwa."

## CHAPTER 1: Blood and Tears

1. Campbell, "The Military Defeat of the South Africans in Angola."
2. South African History Online, "Military Conscription for All White Males in South Africa Is Enforced."
3. Nelson Mandela Foundation, "Historical Background."
4. History.com, "Apartheid."
5. South African Special Forces Association, "General Facts & Figures."
6. Perry, "The Terrible Ones."

## CHAPTER 6: Xhosa Culture

1. Ridley, "We Are the Apes Who Took to the Sea."
2. Lubbe, "Mossel Bay—The True Garden of Eden."

3. Wells, in discussion with the author, March 2016.
4. A1 Jeffreys Bay Accommodation, "Grahamstown History."

## CHAPTER 9: Amayeza

1. Mann, "Negative Ions Create Positive Vibes."

## CHAPTER 11: Call to Ireland

1. Somé, *Of Water and the Spirit.*
2. "An Overview of the History of Pilgrimage to Croagh Patrick."
3. Cooke, "The Holy Mountain That's Become Too Popular."

## CHAPTER 12: Back to Africa

1. Odhav and Naicker, "Mycotoxins in South African Traditionally Brewed Beers."
2. Miyuki, "Self-Realization in the Ten Oxherding Pictures."

## CHAPTER 13: Entering the Shadowlands

1. Vogel, "Great Moments in Comet History: Comet McNaught."

## CHAPTER 15: A Seven-Year Pilgrimage

1. "A Longer History of Druidry."
2. Thornton, *American Indian Holocaust and Survival.*
3. Cultural Survival, Inc., "Huichol."
4. Picken, *Essentials of Shinto,* 226–29.
5. Smyers, *The Fox and the Jewel.*
6. Emoto, *The Hidden Messages in Water.*

## CHAPTER 16: Ubuntu 101 Teachings

1. World Health Organization, "The Top 10 Causes of Death."

# Glossary of Select Terms

*abantu bomlambo*: river people

*amagqirha*: Plural term for Xhosa traditional healers, or sangomas; the ones holding the lightning rod of the ancestors.

*amathambo*: bones

*Camagu!*: This is a powerful word that is used in a variety of ways to honor the observance of the sacred in daily life. It is used as a term of reverence and respect for a Xhosa sangoma. It is also used as an extended "Amen" during traditional ceremonies. In addition, it is uttered when something sacred such as a bird, animal, or event is witnessed.

dreamtime: The time when we are dreaming; it can also refer to the afterlife or spirit/ancestral world.

Cingolweendaba: The name MaMngwevu gave John, meaning "messenger or bridge between people and/or cultures."

*igqirha*: singular term for a Xhosa sangoma

*igqirha elikhulu*: senior sangoma in the Xhosa tradition

*impepho*: a form of African sage

*iindaba*: spiritual news (pl.)

*ingoma*: sangoma song or chant (*iingoma* pl.)

*isilawu*: African herb

*ixhanti*: totem pole

*izinyanya*: Nature spirits, ancestors; the shining ones or the silent hidden ones.

*Karoo*: A semi-desert region of South Africa.

*kraal*: An Afrikaans word referring to a circular structure that is used to hold livestock such as cattle, sheep, goats, etc. It is also used in a spiritual way to connect to the ancestors and uThixo.

*Kyol Che*: A three-month retreat involving meditation, chanting, and bowing.

Mama: A name given to a mother; also a familial term of respect for married women of childbearing age.

*masiy' embo*: let us remember the old ways

sangoma: A traditional South African doctor—shaman and traditional healer.

*sisi*: A young woman, or "sister," not yet married with children.

*Siyavuma!*: We agree!

Tata: A title meaning "father" used for men with children or over the age of forty to show respect.

township: Informal urban area. From the late nineteenth century until the end of apartheid (1994), it was an area reserved for non-white residents.

*thwasa*: the calling illness of the sangoma

*Transkei*: A rural area in the southeastern region of South Africa mainly inhabited by Xhosa-speaking people.

*ubuhlanti*: isiXhosa word for *kraal*. It literally means "the human forest" or "forest of humanity." The place where we reconnect to one another, our ancestors, Great Spirit, and nature.

*Ubuntu*: humanity

*umbilini*: spiritual energy that moves through the spine

*umgoduso*: homecoming ceremony

*umoya*: wind, spirit, or soul

*umoya wezilo*: animal spirits that serve as guardians; shortened form, *isilo* (sing.), *izilo* (pl.)

*umqombothi*: traditional ancestral beer

*umsebenzi*: spiritual work

uThixo: the Great Spirit

*vumisa*: Literally means agreement and is synonymous with the Xhosa divination practice, where it means ancestral agreement.

# Bibliography

A1 Jeffreys Bay Accommodation, "Grahamstown History." a1kynaston.co.za /listing/grahamstown__history.

African National Congress. "A Brief History of the African National Congress." Accessed July 2, 2016. anc.org.za/content/brief-history-anc.

"A Longer History of Druidry." The Order of Bards, Ovates & Druids. druidry.org /druid-way/what-druidry/brief-history-druidry/longer-history-druidry.

"An Overview of the History of Pilgrimage to Croagh Patrick." *Pilgrimage in Medieval Ireland* (blog). Accessed July 20, 2016. pilgrimagemedievalireland .com/2012/07/29/an-overview-of-the-history-of-pilgrimage-to-croagh-patrick/.

Battle, Michael Jesse. *Reconciliation: The Ubuntu Theology of Desmond Tutu.* Rev. ed. Cleveland, OH: Pilgrim Press, 2009.

Bon Yeon. "Obituary—Zen Master Su Bong (1943–1994)." Kwan Um School of Zen. Last modified June 1, 1994. kwanumzen.org /?teaching=obituary-zen-master-su-bong-1943-1994.

Brand South Africa. "Nelson Mandela: A Timeline." Accessed July 22, 2016. brandsouthafrica.com/people-culture/history-heritage /mandela-timeline-december2013.

———. "South Africa's Population." Last modified October 2015. southafrica.info /about/people/population.htm#.V4AY15MrJo4.

Brande, Lauren and Dan Wagener. "About the Alcoholics Anonymous (AA) 12-Step Recovery Program." Recovery.org. August 25, 2016. Last updated December 16, 2015. www.recovery.org/topics/alcoholics-anonymous-12-step/.

Buddha Dharma Education Association. "Masters and Their Organisations: Japanese Zen." Biography of Taisen Deshimaru Roshi. Accessed July 7, 2016. buddhanet.net/masters/deshimaru.htm.

———. "Masters and Their Organisations: Mahayana." Biography of Seung Sahn Soen-sa. Accessed July 9, 2016. buddhanet.net/masters/soen-sa.htm.

Campbell, Horace. "The Military Defeat of the South Africans in Angola." *Monthly Review* 64, no. 11 (April 2013): 32–43. Accessed July 8, 2016. monthlyreview .org/2013/04/01/the-military-defeat-of-the-south-africans-in-angola/.

Cooke, Kieran. "The Holy Mountain That's Become Too Popular." *BBC News Magazine*. October 11, 2015. Accessed July 20, 2016. bbc.com/news /magazine-34475325.

Cultural Survival, Inc. "Huichol." *Cultural Survival Quarterly Magazine*. June 1992. Accessed July 20, 2016. culturalsurvival.org/publications /cultural-survival-quarterly/mexico/huichol.

Dae Bong. "Kyol Che Is Three Great Things." Kwan Um School of Zen. August 6, 2015. Accessed July 24, 2016. kwanumzen.org/kyol-che-is-three-great-things/.

Dae Kwang, ed. *Ten Gates: The Kong-an Teaching of Zen Master Seung Sahn*. Boston: Shambhala Publications, 2007.

Duffell, Nick. *The Making of Them: The British Attitude to Children and the Boarding School System*. London: Lone Arrow Press, 2000.

Emoto, Masaru. *The Hidden Messages in Water*. Translated by David A. Thayne. New York: Atria Books, 2005.

Findley, Lisa, and Liz Ogbu. "South Africa: From Township to Town." *Places Journal*. November 2011. Accessed July 9, 2016. placesjournal.org/article /south-africa-from-township-to-town/.

Flint, Karen. *Healing Traditions: African Medicine, Cultural Exchange, and Competition in South Africa, 1820–1948*. Athens, OH: Ohio University Press, 2008.

Fugelli, Per. "The Healing Dance: Why Society and Medicine Need the General Practitioner." Keynote lecture presented to the Royal Australian College of General Practitioners, 50th Annual Scientific Convention, Sydney, October 5, 2007, 12. Accessed July 20, 2016. folk.uio.no/pfugelli/artikler/healing_dance.pdf.

Grof, Stanislav, and Christina Grof. *Holotropic Breathwork: A New Approach to Self-Exploration and Therapy*. Syracuse: State University of New York Press, 2010.

Hanson, David J. "Historical Evolution of Alcohol Consumption in Society." *Alcohol: Science, Policy and Public Health*. Edited by Peter Boyle et al. Oxford: Oxford University Press, 2013. *Oxford Scholarship Online*. doi: 10.1093/acprof: oso/9780199655786.003.0001.

Highfield, Roger. "Elephants Never Forget Their Dead." *Telegraph*, October 26, 2005. Accessed July 20, 2016. telegraph.co.uk/news/1501489/Elephants-never -forget-their-dead.html.

History.com. "Apartheid." Accessed July 20, 2016. history.com/topics/apartheid.

Irish Department of Education and Skills. "20-Year Strategy for the Irish Language 2010–2030." Accessed July 20, 2016. education.ie/en/The-Education-System /20-Year-Strategy-for-the-Irish-Language/.

James, Kelly, and Ciaran Mac Murchaidh, eds. *Irish and English: Essays on the Irish Linguistic and Cultural Frontier, 1600–1900*. Dublin, Ireland: Four Courts Press, 2012.

Kwan Um School of Zen. "Our Lineage." Accessed July 24, 2016. kwanumzen.org /about-us/our-lineage/.

Lubbe, De Waal. "Mossel Bay—The True Garden of Eden." Accessed April 18, 2017. mosselbayman.co.za/index.php?option=com_content&view=article &id=8h:-genetics-age-of-association-between-helicobacter-pylori-and-modern -thinking-man&catid=2:pages.

Mann, Denise. "Negative Ions Create Positive Vibes." WebMD. May 6, 2002. webmd.com/balance/features/negative-ions-create-positive-vibes#1.

Mayell, Hillary. "Satellites Reveal How Rare Elephants Survive Desert." *National Geographic News*, September 27, 2002. Last updated October 28, 2010. news.nationalgeographic.com/news/2002/09/0927_020927_mali.html.

Miyuki, Mokusen. "Self-Realization in the Ten Oxherding Pictures." *Quadrant* 15, no. 1 (1982).

Mostert, Noel. *Frontiers: The Epic of South Africa's Creation and the Tragedy of the Xhosa People*. New York: Alfred A. Knopf, 1992.

Mqhayi, S. E. K. *Abantu Besizwe: Historical and Biographical Writings, 1902–1944*. Edited and translated by Jeff Opland. Johannesburg, South Africa: Wits University Press, 2009.

National Centers for Environmental Information. "December 26, 2004, Sumatra Indonesia Earthquake and Tsunami." Accessed July 24, 2016. ngdc.noaa.gov /hazard/126dec2004.html.

Nelson Mandela Foundation. "Historical Background: Separate Development." Accessed July 22, 2016. nelsonmandela.org/omalley/cis/omalley/OMalleyWeb /03lv00017/04lv01495/05lv01499.htm.

Odhav, B., and V. Naicker. "Mycotoxins in South African Traditionally Brewed Beers." *Food Additives & Contaminants* 19, no. 1 (2002): 55–61. doi: 10.1080/02652030110053426.

Pappas, John. "Seung Sahn, Explosive Zen and Drunk Angry Monks." *Elephant Journal*, May 4, 2010. elephantjournal.com/2010/05 /seung-sahn-explosive-zen-and-drunk-angry-monks/.

Perry, Mike. "The Terrible Ones: South Africa's '32 Battalion.'" *SpecialOperations.com* (blog). January 20, 2014. Accessed July 20, 2016. specialoperations.com/28703 /terrible-ones-south-africas-32-battalion/.

Peters, Larry G. "An Experiential Study of Nepalese Shamanism." In *Shamanism: Critical Concepts in Sociology*, vol. 1. Edited by Andrei A. Znamenski. London: Routledge, 2004.

Picken, Stuart D. B. *Essentials of Shinto: An Analytical Guide to Principal Teachings*. Westport, CT: Greenwood Press, 1994.

Ridley, Matt. "We Are the Apes Who Took to the Sea." *Wall Street Journal*, March 12, 2011.

Seung Sahn. *The Compass of Zen*. Boston: Shambhala Publications, 1997.

Shambhala International. "Buddhism." Accessed July 20, 2016. shambhala.org /about-shambhala/the-shambhala-path/buddhism/.

Sharlet, Jeff. "Inside Occupy Wall Street." *Rolling Stone*, November 10, 2011. Accessed July 20, 2016. rollingstone.com/politics/news /occupy-wall-street-welcome-to-the-occupation-20111110.

Shkala, Anna-Leena. "Siberian and Inner Shamanism." *Shamanism: Critical Concepts in Sociology*, vol. 1. Edited by Andrei A. Znamenski. London: Routledge, 2004.

Smyers, Karen A. *The Fox and the Jewel: Shared and Private Meanings in Contemporary Japanese Inari Worship*. Honolulu: University of Hawaii Press, 1999.

Somé, Malidoma Patrice. *Of Water and the Spirit: Ritual, Magic, and Initiation in the Life of an African Shaman*. London: Penguin Books, 1995.

South Africa Department of Information and Publicity. "Statement on Battalion 32's Rampage through Phola Park." April, 10, 1992. Accessed July 20, 2016. web.archive.org/web/20080708193835/http://www.anc.org.za/ancdocs /pr/1992/pr0410a.html.

South African History Online. "Military Conscription for All White Males in South Africa Is Enforced." August 4, 1967. Last modified July 31, 2013. sahistory.org .za/dated-event/military-conscription-all-white-males-south-africa-enforced.

———. "Second Anglo-Boer War 1899–1902." Last modified August 16, 2016. sahistory.org.za/article/second-anglo-boer-war-1899-1902.

———. "Vusamazulu Credo Mutwa." Accessed July 20, 2017. sahistory.org.za /people/vusamazulu-credo-mutwa.

South African Special Forces Association. "General Facts & Figures." Accessed July 20, 2016. recce.co.za/training-and-operations/facts-and-figures.

Steadman, Lyle B., Craig T. Palmer, and Christopher F. Tilley. "The Universality of Ancestor Worship." *Ethnology* 35, no. 1 (1996): 63–76.

Stearns, Peter N., ed. *The Encyclopedia of World History: Ancient, Medieval, and Modern—Chronologically Arranged*. 6th ed. Cambridge, England: James Clarke & Co, 2002.

Sternbeg, Leo. "Extracts from Divine Election in Primitive Religion." In *Shamanism: Critical Concepts in Sociology*, vol. 1. Edited by Andrei A. Znamenski. London: Routledge, 2004.

Su Bong Zen Monastery. "Zen Master Su Bong." Accessed July 8, 2016. subong.org.hk/en/teaching/3.

Tanahashi, Kazuaki. *The Heart Sutra: A Comprehensive Guide to the Classic of Mahayana Buddhism*. Boulder, CO: Shambhala Publications, 2016.

Thornton, Russell. *American Indian Holocaust and Survival: A Population History Since 1492*. The Civilization of the American Indian Series, vol. 186. Norman: University of Oklahoma Press, 1990.

Traill, Anthony. "Khoisan Languages." *Encyclopedia Britannica Online*. Accessed July 8, 2016. britannica.com/topic/Khoisan-languages.

Vogel, Tracy. "Great Moments in Comet History: Comet McNaught." *ISONblog* (blog). *HubbleSite*. July 16, 2013. Accessed July 20, 2016. hubblesite.org/hubble_discoveries /comet_ison/blogs/great-moments-in-comet-history-comet-mcnaught.

Wells, Julie (professor of history, Rhodes University, Grahamstown, South Africa). Discussion with the author, March 2016.

Western Reserve Public Media. "The Middle Ages." Accessed July 20, 2016. westernreservepublicmedia.org/middleages/feud_nobles.htm.

World Health Organization. "The Top 10 Causes of Death." Updated January 2017. who.int/mediacentre/factsheets/fs310/en/.

Wu Bong. "On the Five Precepts." Kwan Um School of Zen. Accessed July 24, 2016. kwanumzen.org/?teaching=on-the-five-precepts.

Yogananda, Paramahansa. "Kundalini Awakening." Excerpts from *The Second Coming of Christ*. Accessed July 25, 2016. yogananda.com.au/sc/sc14 _kundalini1.html.

# Further Information

John runs The Way of the Leopard retreats in South Africa, Europe, Ireland, and the United States, with plans to expand this offering to other areas of the world. These retreats focus on the importance of helping people connect to their inner wildness and thus realize their calling in the world, and essential humanity (Ubuntu), through observing nature. He guides people through a process of dream work, medicinal plant cleanses, heartbeat meditation, trance dancing, and teaches the ancient art of prayer through honoring ancestors. For further information about his work and events schedule, please visit johnlockley.com or facebook.com/JohnLockley777.

# About the Author

John Lockley is a traditionally trained Xhosa sangoma—known locally as an igqirha, a traditional healer, or shaman—from South Africa. He is the founder of The Way of the Leopard teachings which are inspired by his Zen training and sangoma apprenticeship. John is a pioneer in bridging ancient South African healing technology—sangoma medicine—with the mainstream, Western medical culture.

John has practiced meditation in the Zen Buddhist tradition for more than twenty-five years. He studied under Zen Master Su Bong in South Korea.

John's background in general/clinical psychology has been a crucial influence in his path to help heal emotional, psychological, and physical trauma.

In addition to teaching and public speaking, John has a busy private practice as a traditional healer and diviner, offering spiritual counseling to help people connect with their intrinsic humanity (Ubuntu), to achieve their full potential. As a modern mystic, he does this through an intricate exploration of ancestors and family relationships, "bone-throwing" divination, and dreams.

John continues his work in traditional sangoma communities across South Africa, and runs workshops and retreats worldwide. *Leopard Warrior* is his first book.

# About Sounds True

Sounds True is a multimedia publisher whose mission is to inspire and support personal transformation and spiritual awakening. Founded in 1985 and located in Boulder, Colorado, we work with many of the leading spiritual teachers, thinkers, healers, and visionary artists of our time. We strive with every title to preserve the essential "living wisdom" of the author or artist. It is our goal to create products that not only provide information to a reader or listener, but that also embody the quality of a wisdom transmission.

For those seeking genuine transformation, Sounds True is your trusted partner. At SoundsTrue.com you will find a wealth of free resources to support your journey, including exclusive weekly audio interviews, free downloads, interactive learning tools, and other special savings on all our titles.

To learn more, please visit SoundsTrue.com/freegifts or call us toll-free at 800.333.9185.

SOUNDS TRUE
many voices, one journey